FOREWORD BY LEWIS HOWES

The

MIRACLE MORNING

for ENTREPRENEURS

Elevate Yourself To
Elevate Your Business

Hal Elrod • Cameron Herold

With Honorée Corder

THE MIRACLE MORNING FOR ENTREPRENEURS

Hal Elrod & Cameron Herold
with Honorée Corder

Interior Design: Christina Gorchos, 3CsBooks.com

ISBN-13: 978-1942589129

ENDORSEMENTS

"I had been a night owl almost all of my life, until I finally discovered the Miracle Morning and soon realized the power of starting my day with purpose. As an entrepreneur, it's been incredibly helpful as it has massively increased my productivity, creativity and focus. If you're not reading this book, you're not ever going to be as successful as you can be." —**Pat Flynn,** *Wall Street Journal* **best-selling author of** *Will It Fly?* **and host of the #1 rated** *Smart Passive Income* **Podcast**

"Success leaves clues. What is one shift, one idea could dramatically up level your business and your life? The Miracle Morning is that idea and the secret habit used by a multitude of successful entrepreneurs." —**JJ Virgin, founder of JJ Virgin & Associates and Mindshare Collaborative**

"Entrepreneurs are the creators and visionaries of this world and too often we think we need a blank canvas to do that. But I've learned that adding structure and a positive routine, especially first-thing in the morning, is critical to getting your big dreams accomplished. Even if you're not a 'morning person' this is the blueprint you need to get great things done." —**Yanik Silver, author** *Evolved Enterprise* **and founder of Maverick1000**

"This is the book that I wish I had in my back pocket, torn and tattered, with my notes all over it, 15 years ago. It would have saved me a lot of grief. I've been lucky enough to find these principles in my life and become a successful entrepreneur since then. But Cameron lays it all out and cracks the code so everyone can see. This is a great book for entrepreneurs or the many people who will be successful becoming an entrepreneur." —**James Altucher, founder of Choose Yourself Media**

"There's a saying that if you win the morning, you've won the day... Authored by two of the smartest business minds I know, *The Miracle Morning for Entrepreneurs* is a playbook for those who want to take their mornings (and their businesses) to the next level!" —**Jayson Gaignard, founder of MastermindTalks**

"Hal and Cameron's newest book shows you that not all morning routines are created equally. Any entrepreneur can benefit from these frameworks to start your day with your best foot forward." —**Ari Meisel, founder of Less Doing**

"As an entrepreneur, you're always trying to take resources from a lower level of productivity to a higher level. Inside Cameron Herold and Hal Elrod's new book, *The Morning Miracle for Entrepreneurs*, you'll discover how to develop a bigger and better vision for your business, how to master your mornings, how to better manage your energy and take your success to a higher level. Read this book now if you want to become an even more influential and inspiring entrepreneur." —**Joe Polish, Founder of Genius Network and Piranha Marketing Inc.**

"Many entrepreneurs loathe the morning. That's easy to understand given how many of us work well into the night and even into the sunrise the following day. To be honest, I don't have the most consistent of morning routines. But when I do start the day off right, everything seems to move more smoothly. If you're looking for inspiration and guidance on how to begin each day with a spring in your step, ready to conquer anything that comes your way, look no further than *The Miracle Morning*. Filled with techniques and tactics for maximizing your mornings (and the rest of your day for that matter) *The Miracle Morning for Entrepreneurs* is the perfect guide to starting your day off right and keeping things running smoothly until you head to bed." —**Joey Coleman, Chief Experience Composer of Design Symphony**

DEDICATION

HAL

This book, in particular, I dedicate to my fellow entrepreneurs—those of us who have been at this game for a long time, as well as those of you who are just starting out—I admire you for your courage to venture out into the unknown, to create value for the world and freedom for you and your family.

However, none of us succeed on our own. Supporting every great entrepreneur is a circle of influence that has helped to shape our journey and often been the reason why we're willing to put in so many hours.

At the center of my circle is my wife, Ursula, the woman of my dreams, whose support makes the work I do possible. Thank you for believing in me when I didn't believe in myself. To our children, Sophie and Halsten, you inspire me to do more, be more, and create more, and I love you more than anything in this world.

Lastly, I'd like to thank Cameron Herold for working with me to co-create this book. I was a fan of Cameron long before we ever met in person, so it's been an honor to put our heads together and co-author what we believe will be a game changer for you.

CAMERON

I would like to thank all the entrepreneurs and CEOs I've formally coached over the last decade. Your routines and thirst for learning have inspired me to grow as well.

Most importantly, my wife, Kimberley, who is the most amazing woman I've ever met—I'm blessed—and I'd be lost without her. Also, to our four kids, Aidan, Connor, Hannah, and Emily—thank you for letting me pursue my business dreams, which gives me the free time to make memories with all of you. I love you all!

CONTENTS

Section I: The Miracle Morning + Life S.A.V.E.R.S.

    The case for mornings and why they are critically important
    to a entrepreneur's success (and what happens when you
    don't take advantage of them).

    Even if you've never been a morning person, here's the most
    effective way to overcome the challenges of waking up early,
    beat the snooze button, and maximize your mornings.

    Harness the life-changing power of the most effective,
    proven personal development practices known to man,
    which are guaranteed to save you from missing out on the
    levels of success (in every area of your life) that you truly
    want and deserve.

Section II: The Entrepreneur's Elevation Skills

    Discover why who you're becoming is significatly more
    important than what you say and do each day, and precisely
    how to lead yourself to the next level so you can take your
    success to the next level (because it only happens in that
    order).

Section III: The Entrepreneurial Elevation Principles

A SPECIAL INVITATION FROM HAL

Readers and practitioners of *The Miracle Morning* have co-created an extraordinary community consisting of over 200,000 like-minded individuals, from around the world, who wake up each day *with purpose* and dedicate time to fulfilling the unlimited potential that is within all of us while helping others to do the same.

As author of *The Miracle Morning*, I felt that I had a responsibility to create an online community where readers could come together to connect, get encouragement, share best practices, support one another, discuss the book, post videos, find accountability partners, and even swap smoothie recipes and exercise routines.

However, I honestly had no idea that The Miracle Morning Community would become one of the most positive, engaged, and supportive online communities in the world, but it has. I'm constantly astounded by the caliber, and the character of our members, which presently includes people from over 70 countries and is growing daily.

Just go to **www.MyTMMCommunity.com** and request to join The Miracle Morning Community on Facebook®. You'll immediately be able to connect with 80,000+ people who are already practicing TMM. While you'll find many who are just beginning their Miracle Morning journey, you'll find even more who have been at it for years, and who will happily share advice, support, and guidance to accelerate your success.

I'll be moderating the Community and checking in regularly, so I look forward to seeing you there! If you'd like to reach out to me personally on social media, follow **@HalElrod** on Twitter and **Facebook.com/YoPalHal** on Facebook. Let's connect soon!

FOREWORD

By Lewis Howes,
New York Times Best-selling author of
The School of Greatness

Choosing to be an entrepreneur is easily one of the most challenging career paths someone can select. Behind the allure of freedom, flexibility, uncapped potential, and living the dream, lies a cold reality. That reality includes countless long days that turn into late nights, week after week, year after year. Uncertainty, second-guessing, failures, mistakes, and disappointments are all part of the entrepreneur's journey.

But entrepreneurs choose to stick with this self-imposed Mt. Everest climb because they know what they're capable of. And the impact they make on the world is worth all the challenges.

However, entrepreneurship does not have to be as taxing as many people paint it to be. If you commit to the habits and priorities that support you in functioning at your very best every day, you can bypass so much of the stress, fatigue, and overwhelm that plagues the majority of entrepreneurs.

As a former two sport All-American, professional football player, and current US Men's National Team Handball player, I learned early on that the habits I had in place as an athlete and entrepreneur determine the success of my dreams.

The Miracle Morning for Entrepreneurs is the ultimate real-world playbook to which habits and what priorities will allow you to achieve your dreams. It's a perfect compass to point you in the direction of what to put at the top of your list—every day—to ensure you climb the heights of entrepreneurship with confidence and lasting energy. There's no better way to set yourself up to win than by investing in these positive daily habits. If you do, the allures of entrepreneurship and fulfillment will become your reality.

Signed,

Lewis Howes

LewisHowes.com

A NOTE FROM HAL

Welcome to the Miracle Morning. I think it's safe for us to say that there is at least one thing we have in common (probably a lot more than just *one*, but at least one that we know for sure): *We want to improve our lives and ourselves.* This is not to suggest that there is anything necessarily "wrong" with us, or our lives, but as human beings, we were born with the innate desire and drive to continuously grow and improve. I believe it's within all of us. Yet, most of us wake up each day, and life pretty much stays the same.

Whatever your life is like right now—whether you are currently experiencing extraordinary levels of success, enduring the most challenging time of your life, or somewhere in between—I can say with absolute certainty that the Miracle Morning is the most practical, results-oriented, and effective method I have ever encountered for improving **every** area of your life and doing so faster than you may believe is possible.

For achievers and top performers, the Miracle Morning can be an absolute game-changer, allowing you to attain that elusive *next level* and take your personal and professional success far beyond what you've achieved up to this point. While this can include increasing your income or growing your business, sales, and revenue, it's often more about discovering new ways to experience deeper levels of fulfillment and success in aspects of your life that you may have neglected. This can mean making significant improvements in your **health**, **happiness**, **relationships**, **finances**, **spirituality**, or any other areas that are at the top of your list.

For those who are in the midst of adversity and enduring times of struggle—be it mental, emotional, physical, financial, relational, or other—the Miracle Morning has proven time and time again to be the one thing that can empower anyone to overcome seemingly insurmountable challenges, make major breakthroughs, and turn their circumstances around, often in a short period of time.

Whether you want to make significant improvements in just a few key areas, or you are ready for a major overhaul that will radically transform your entire life—so that your current circumstances will soon become a memory of what was—you've picked up the right book. You are about to begin a miraculous journey using a simple, step-by-step process that is guaranteed to transform any area of your life ... all before 8:00 a.m.

I know, I know—these are some big promises to make. But the Miracle Morning is already generating measurable results for hundreds of thousands of people around the world, and it can absolutely be the one thing that takes you to where you want to be. My co-authors and I have done everything in our power to ensure that this book will be a truly life-changing investment of your time, energy, and attention. Thank you for allowing us to be a part of your life. Our miraculous journey together is about to begin.

With love & gratitude,

Hal

A NOTE FROM CAMERON HEROLD:

My Miracle Morning

What greater wealth is there than to own your life
and to spend it on growing? Every living thing must grow.
It can't stand still. It must grow or perish.
—AYN RAND, *Atlas Shrugged*

Hal and the original *Miracle Morning* changed my life. Adopting the morning routine, I found in that book led me to become a stronger entrepreneur so that I can help the CEOs I mentor to adopt routines to take themselves and their businesses to a level they never thought possible.

In *The 7 Habits of Highly Effective People*, Stephen Covey talks about the importance of prioritizing the activities that are important but not urgent in lieu of more urgent (and less important) tasks. He defines important activities as the things that are critical to accomplishing your long-term goals, but have no inherent deadline.

The tools in this book, and many that I use on my best days, are just that. And the more often I do them, the better life gets.

My miracle mornings consist of a routine that includes mindfulness, my gratitude journal, meditation, easing into my day without looking at my email, and a host of health supplements like vitamins, probiotics, lemon juice, garlic, and tea (instead of coffee).

How We Got Here

Hal and I met some time ago through a couple of mastermind groups we both belong to. I was consciously focusing on raising my business game yet again, but it was Hal's focus on personal growth and this morning routine that caught my attention.

When my wife first told me about *The Miracle Morning* years ago, I thought *nope! I'm definitely not a morning person* and continued my normal routine of hitting the snooze button.

Eventually, *The Miracle Morning* started going viral. I saw people I know post about how it had changed their lives. I thought *this Miracle Morning thing seems to be catching on ... good for Hal!* Needless to say, I had to read it, I loved it, and I implemented it. And now I'm training for my first marathon in addition to being the weight I was 20 years ago. When Hal reached out to me and asked if I'd be interested in co-authoring this book, I felt honored. And the result, of course, you now hold in your hand. In addition to Hal and I coming together for this book, I interviewed other top-producing entrepreneurs and their profiles are included.

The Miracle Morning for Entrepreneurs

If you want to attract, create, and sustain extraordinary levels of success and income, you must first figure out how to *become the person* that is capable of easily and consistently attracting, creating, and sustaining the extraordinary levels of success and income that you desire.

Then, you must master what the top entrepreneurs know about building a business that provides the freedom and income only the top 1 percent enjoy.

The Miracle Morning for Entrepreneurs is not like any other book on entrepreneurship. It's *the* reference book that reveals how to succeed in *every* area of your life, simultaneously: how to be a top entrepreneur *and* experience a life of health, balance, and fulfillment. This is a book that tells you what the top entrepreneurs do, and it gives you an edge, right from the start, by helping you to become one of them—mentally, emotionally, spiritually, skillfully, *and* strategically.

It's Your Turn

What if you could wake up effortlessly in the morning, equipped with extraordinary levels of energy, clarity, and the unwavering focus you need to execute your highest priorities and take yourself, and your business to the next level? What if waking up early was a habit you absolutely loved? What if every morning could feel like Christmas morning—you know, the really awesome Christmas mornings of your childhood? When you went to bed filled with so much anticipation and excitement of what would happen the next day, you practically ripped your covers off the next morning to get on with the business of ripping open all your gifts! (Or was that just me?) Any interest?

I can assure you that's exactly how I feel each and every day. I go to bed looking forward to the next day and wake up each morning anticipating what the day has in store for me. I'm utterly grateful my life has transformed into something so amazing.

I know. You might be thinking, *I've tried and failed. I've tried to get up earlier. I've tried to master my life and my professional growth. I have failed more times than I care to admit, and I'm nervous about trying something new. Can this really help me?*

Yes! Yes! *Yes!*

I believe that to be truly successful, in whatever way you measure success, you must master both your inner and outer game. It all starts with the morning. When you own the morning, you own the day. And when you own the day, you own your entrepreneurial journey.

If you let it, *The Miracle Morning for Entrepreneurs* can be your coach, accountability partner, and mastermind team rolled into one.

Keep this book and your journal close at hand so you can read it, revisit it, make notes, jot down the distinctions you make, and track your progress.

You can be just as successful, if not more so, than I have been. You can take the success I've enjoyed and multiply it for yourself.

It all starts with taking control of your mornings. Are you ready?

SECTION 1:

THE MIRACLE MORNING
+
LIFE S.A.V.E.R.S

—1—

WHY MORNINGS MATTER

(MORE THAN YOU THINK)

*Your first ritual that you do during the day is the highest
leveraged ritual by far, because it has the effect of setting your
mind, and setting the context, for the rest of your day.*
—EBEN PAGAN

How you start each morning determines your mindset and the context for the rest of your day. Begin with a purposeful, disciplined, growth-infused, and goal-oriented morning, and you're virtually guaranteed to crush the day.

Do you wake up feeling overwhelmed? I'd be willing to bet that most entrepreneurs do. Their day starts with procrastination, hitting the snooze button, and sending a message to their subconscious mind that says they don't have enough self-discipline to get out of bed, let alone do what's necessary to reach their business growth goals.

But what if you could change it?

What if you could start your day with an hour of peace and quiet? An uncluttered mental space where you could regain your sense of calm focus, where you're in total control and can proceed in an orderly, self-nurturing fashion? But you know you can't—or maybe you can but not today.

What if, when the alarm goes off in the morning, you could consider it to be life's first gift? It's the gift of time you can dedicate to becoming the person you need to be to achieve all your goals and dreams—for yourself and your business—while the rest of the world is still asleep.

While most entrepreneurs wake up and think they need to focus on *doing* more so they can achieve more, you're about to discover that the real secret is all about *becoming* more so that you can achieve more by doing *less*.

You might be thinking, *All of this sounds great, Cameron. But. I. Am. Not. A. Morning. Person.*

I understand. I really do! You're not saying anything I haven't told myself a thousand times before. And believe me, I tried—and failed—many times to take control of my mornings. But that was before I discovered *The Miracle Morning*.

Stay with me for a minute. In addition to wanting to have the biggest and best company possible, I bet you also want to stop struggling and worrying about having more month than money, quit missing your goals, and release all the intense and not-so-great emotions that go along with those challenges. Right? These things get in the way of being an effective entrepreneur because they affect your self-esteem and prevent you from feeling good about your-self and your life, which keeps you from taking effective action in pursuit of your goals.

Sound familiar?

Then know this: *Mornings are the key to it all.*

More important than even the *time* that you start your day is the *mindset* with which you start your day.

Maybe your dream is to build a substantial income with your company so you can inspect your alarm clock's insides with a baseball bat and see what it's like to start your day on *your* time for a while.

Trust me, I get it, and I often decide to start my day whenever I wake up naturally. However, even when I do that, my Miracle Morning is the first part of my day and gets me in the right mindset to make the most of my time.

Plus, there is a good chance that you're reading this book in the early stages of being an entrepreneur, which means that you are probably building your company from before the sun rises until long after it sets. If that's the case, then learning to implement your Miracle Morning is going to be critical to exploding your life as an entrepreneur so that you can finally realize the success you envision. Here's the good news ... implementing a miracle morning practice is worth it, and it is far more fun and rewarding than you might expect.

But, before we get into exactly *how* you can master your mornings, let me make the case for *why*. Because believe me, once you know the truth about mornings, you'll never want to miss one again.

Why Mornings Matter So Much

The more you explore the power of early rising and morning rituals, the more the proof mounts that the early bird gets *a lot* more than the worm. Here are just a few of the key advantages you're about to experience for yourself.

You'll be more proactive and productive.

Christoph Randler is a professor of biology at the University of Education in Heidelberg, Germany. In the July 2010 issue of *Harvard Business Review*, Randler found that "People whose performance peaks in the morning are better positioned for career success, because they're more proactive than people who are at their best in the evening." According to *New York Times* best-selling author and world renowned entrepreneur Robin Sharma, "If you study many of the most productive people in the world, they all had one thing in common—they were early risers."

You'll anticipate problems and head them off at the pass.

Randler went on to surmise that morning people hold all the important cards. They are "better able to anticipate and minimize problems, are proactive, have greater professional success and ultimately make higher wages." He noted that morning people are able to anticipate problems and handle them with grace and ease, which makes them better in business.

You'll plan like a pro.

Morning folks have the time to organize, anticipate, and plan for their day. Our sleepy counterparts are reactive rather than proactive, leaving a lot to chance. Aren't you more stressed when you sleep through your alarm or wake up late? Getting up with the sun (or before) lets you jump-start your day. While everyone else is running around trying (and failing) to get their day under control, you'll be calm, cool, and collected.

You'll have more energy.

One component of your new Miracle Mornings will be exercise, which is often neglected by busy entrepreneurs. Yet, in as little as just a few minutes, exercise sets a positive tone for the day. Increased blood flow to the brain will help you think more clearly and focus on what's most important. Fresh oxygen will permeate every cell in your body and increase your energy all day, which is why top entrepreneurs who exercise report being in a better mood and in better shape, getting better sleep, and being more productive. This, of course, will result in your producing significant increases in your numbers. You'll acquire more customers, find better employees, and grow a better business!

You'll gain early bird attitude advantages.

Recently, researchers at the University of Barcelona in Spain compared morning people, those early birds who like to get up at dawn, with evening people, night owls who prefer to stay up late and sleep in. Among the differences, they found that morning people tend to be more persistent and resistant to fatigue, frustration, and difficulties. That translates into lower levels of anxiety, rates of depression, and less likelihood of substance abuse but higher life satisfaction. Sounds good to me.

The evidence is in, and the experts have had their say. *Mornings contain the secret to an extraordinarily successful future in entrepreneurship.*

Mornings? Really?

I'll admit it. To go from *I'm not a morning person* to *I really want to become a morning person* to *I'm up early every morning, and it feels amazing!* is a process. But after some trial and error, you will discover how to out-fox, pre-empt, and foil your inner late sleeper so you can make early rising a habit. Okay, sounds great in theory, but you might be shaking your head and telling yourself, *There's no way. I'm already cramming 27 hours of stuff into 24 hours. How on earth could I get up an hour earlier than I already do?* I ask, how can you not?

The key thing to understand is that the Miracle Morning isn't about trying to deny yourself another hour of sleep so you can have an even longer, harder day. It's not even about waking up earlier. It's about waking up *better.*

Thousands of people around the planet are already living their own Miracle Mornings. Many of them were night owls. But they're making it work. In fact, they're *thriving.* And it's not because they simply added an hour to their day. It's because they added *the right* hour. And so can you.

Still skeptical? Then let me tell you this: *The hardest part about getting up an hour earlier is the first five minutes.* That's the crucial time when, tucked into your warm bed, you make the decision to start your day or hit the snooze button *just one more time.* It's the moment of truth, and the decision you make right then will change your day, your success, and your life.

And that's why that first five minutes is the starting point for *The Miracle Morning for Entrepreneurs.* It's time for you to win every morning! When we win our mornings, we win the day.

In the next two chapters, I'll make waking up early easier and more exciting than it's ever been in your life (even if you've *never* considered yourself to be a morning person), and then I'll show you how to maximize those newfound morning minutes with the Life S.A.V.E.R.S. for Entrepreneurs—the six most powerful, proven personal development practices known to man.

Chapters 4, 5, and 6 will give you the entrepreneur's elevation skills related to accelerating your personal and professional growth, why you need to strategically engineer your life for endless amounts of energy, and how to optimize your ability to remain focused on your goals and the activities that generate the greatest returns.

Finally, chapters 7, 8, and 9 cover the entrepreneurial elevation principles you must master to become a successful entrepreneur, elevate your business, and increase your income as fast as humanly possible. There's even a final bonus chapter from Hal and me that I think you are really going to love!

We have a lot of ground to cover in this book, so let's jump right in.

Entrepreneur Profile

Joe Polish

Joe Polish is the founder of Genius Network and Piranha Marketing Inc.

Top Business Accomplishments

- ❖ Joe curates the highest level network in the world for successful entrepreneurs, called Genius Network, in which more than 240 entrepreneurs invest $25,000 a year.

- ❖ Millions of people have downloaded his podcasts at ILoveMarketing.com and 10XTalk.com.

- ❖ He has raised more than $3 million for Richard Branson's charity Virgin Unite.

- ❖ He came up with the idea for JoeVolunteer.com, which is like Uber for volunteers, that is transforming the way people do good work in the world.

- ❖ He co-founded www.ArtistsForAddicts.com to help change the way the world views and treats people with addictions.

Morning Routine

- ❖ Joe wakes between 6:00 and 7:00 a.m.

- ❖ Within 30 minutes, he drinks a smoothie and a big glass of water.

- ❖ Then he spends time in meditation.

- ❖ For exercise, Joe lifts weights or does yoga.

❖ Then he checks in with his team, including his awesome assistant, Eunice.

❖ He uses the CommitTo3 app with Cameron and lists three things he wants to get done during the day.

❖ Because he self-identifies as an addict, recovery work is an important part of his routine. On any given day, that could involve a phone call, talking, journaling, reading, or listening to something positive.

IT ONLY TAKES FIVE MINUTES TO BECOME A MORNING PERSON

If you really think about it, hitting the snooze button in the morning doesn't even make sense. It's like saying, "I hate getting up in the morning, so I do it over, and over, and over again."
—DEMETRI MARTIN, Comedian

I t is possible to love waking up—even if you've *never* been a morning person.

I know you might not believe it. Right now you might think *that might be true for early birds, but trust me, I've tried. I'm just not a morning person.*

But it's true. I know because I've been there. I was a bleary-eyed, snooze-button pusher. A "snooze-aholic" as Hal calls it. I dreaded mornings. I hated waking up.

And now I love it.

How did I do it? When people ask me how I transformed myself into a morning person—and transformed my life in the process—I tell them I did it in five simple steps, one at a time. I know it may seem downright impossible. But take it from a former snooze-aholic: You can do this. And you can do it the same way that I did.

That's the critical message about waking up—it's possible to change. Morning people aren't born—they're self-made. You can become a morning person, and you can do it in simple steps that don't require the willpower of an Olympic marathoner. I contend that when early rising becomes not something you do but *who you are*, you will truly love mornings. Waking up will become for you like it is for me, not quite effortless, but moments after getting out of bed I'm already energized knowing what's about to take place.

Not convinced? Suspend your disbelief (just a little) and let me introduce you to the five-step process that changed my life. Five simple, snooze-proof keys made waking up in the morning— even early in the morning—easier than ever before. Without this strategy, I would still be sleeping (or snoozing) through my alarm(s) each morning. Worse, I would still be clinging to the limiting belief that I am not a morning person.

And I would have missed a whole world of opportunity.

The Challenge with Waking Up

Waking up earlier is a bit like running: You think you're not a runner—maybe you even *hate* running—until you lace up a pair of running shoes and reluctantly head out the front door at a pace that suggests you might be about to go for a run. With a commitment to overcome your seemingly insurmountable disdain for running, you put one foot in front of the other. Do this for a few weeks, and one day, it hits you: *I've become a runner.*

Similarly, if you've resisted waking up in the morning and chosen to hit the *procrastination* button—I mean *snooze* button, then of course you're not *yet* a morning person. But follow the simple steps-by-step process that you're about to discover, and you'll wake up in a few weeks (maybe even a few days) and it will hit you: *OMG, I can't believe it ... I've become a morning person!*

The possibilities feel amazing right now, and you might be feeling motivated, excited, optimistic. But what happens tomorrow morning when that alarm goes off? How motivated will you be when you're yanked out of a deep sleep by a screaming alarm clock?

We all know where motivation will be right then. It will be flushed down the toilet and have been replaced by rationalization. And rationalization is a crafty master—in seconds, we can convince ourselves that we need just a few extra minutes ... and the next thing we know, we're scrambling around the house late for work, late for life. Again.

It's a tricky problem. Just when we need our motivation the most—those first few moments of the day—is precisely when we seem to have the least of it.

The solution is to boost that morning motivation and mount a surprise attack on rationalization. That's what the five steps that follow do for you. Each step in the process is designed to increase what Hal calls your Wake Up Motivation Level (WUML).

First thing in the morning, you might have a low WUML, meaning you want nothing more than to go back to sleep when your alarm goes off. That's normal. But by using this simple five-step process (which takes about five minutes), you can generate a high WUML that makes you ready to jump up and embrace the day.

The Five-Step, Snooze-Proof, Wake-Up Strategy

Minute One: Set Your Intentions Before Bed

The first key to waking up is to understand this: *Your first thought in the morning is usually the same as your last thought before you went to sleep.* I bet, for example, that you've had nights where you could hardly fall asleep because you were so excited about waking up the next morning. Whether it was when you were a kid on Christmas morning, or the day you were leaving for a big vacation, as soon as the alarm sounded, you opened your eyes ready to jump out of bed. Why? It's because the last thought you had about the coming morning—before you fell asleep—was positive.

On the other hand, if your last thought before bed is, "Oh gosh, I can't believe I have to get up in six hours—I'm going to be exhausted in the morning!" then your first thought when the alarm clock goes off is likely to be something like, "Oh gosh, it's already been six hours? Nooo … I just want to keep sleeping!" consider that it is a self-fulfilling prophecy and that you create your own reality.

The first step is to consciously decide—every night, before bed—to actively and mindfully create a positive expectation for the next morning. Visualize it and affirm it to yourself.

For help on this and to get the precise words to say before bed to create your powerful morning intentions, download "The Miracle Morning Bedtime Affirmations" free at www.TMMBook.com.

Minute Two: Move Your Alarm Clock Across the Room

If you haven't already, be sure to move your alarm clock as far away from your bed as possible. This will make it so you have to actually get out of bed and engage your body in movement to start each day. Motion creates energy, and getting out of bed and walking across the room naturally helps you to wake up.

Most people keep their alarm clock next to their bed. Think about it: if you keep your alarm clock within reach, then you're still in a partial sleep state after the alarm goes off, and your wake up motivation level (a.k.a. your WUML) is at its lowest point, which makes it much more difficult to summon the discipline to get out of bed. In fact, you may turn off the alarm without even realizing it! On more than a few occasions, we've all convinced ourselves that our alarm clock was merely part of the dream we were having. (You're not alone on that one, trust me.)

By forcing yourself to get out of bed to turn off the alarm, you are setting yourself up for early rising success by instantly increasing your WUML.

However, on a scale of one to ten, your WUML may still be hovering around five, and you'll likely be feeling sleepier than not, so the temptation to turn around and crawl back into bed will still be present. To raise that WUML just a little further, try ...

Minute Three: Brush Your Teeth

As soon as you've gotten out of bed and turned off your alarm clock, go directly to the bathroom sink to brush your teeth. I know what you may be thinking. *Really? You're telling me that I need to brush my teeth?* Yes. The point is that you're doing mindless activities for the first few minutes and giving your body time to wake up.

After turning off your alarm, go directly to the bathroom sink to brush your teeth and splash some warm (or cold) water on your face. This simple activity will allow for the passing of more time to increase your WUML even further.

Now that your mouth is minty fresh, it's time to ...

Minute Four: Drink a Full Glass of Water

It's crucial that you hydrate yourself first thing every morning. After six to eight hours without water, you'll be mildly dehydrated, which causes fatigue. Often when people feel tired—at any time of day—what they really need is more water, not more sleep.

Start by getting a glass or bottle of water (or you can do what I do and fill it up the night before so it's already there for you in the morning) and drinking it as fast as is comfortable for you. The objective is to replace the water you were deprived of during the hours you slept. (And hey, the side benefits of morning hydration include better, younger-looking skin and maintaining a healthy weight. Not bad for a few ounces of water!)

That glass of water should raise your WUML another notch, which will get you to ...

Minute Five: Get Dressed in Your Workout Clothes (or Jump in the Shower)

The fifth step has two options. *Option one* is to get dressed in your exercise clothing so you're ready to leave your bedroom and immediately engage in your Miracle Morning. You can lay out your clothes before you go to bed or sleep in your workout clothes. (Yes, really.) You can make this part of your bedtime ritual.

Option two is to jump in the shower, which is a great way to take your WUML to the point where staying awake is much easier. However, I usually opt to change into exercise clothes, since I'll need a shower after working out, and I believe there is something to be said for *earning* your morning shower! But a lot of people prefer their shower first because it helps them wake up and gives them a fresh start to the day. The choice is completely yours.

Regardless of which option you choose, by the time you've executed these five simple steps, your WUML should be high enough that it requires very little discipline to stay awake for your Miracle Morning.

If you were to try to make that commitment the moment your alarm first went off—while you were at a WUML of nearly zero—it would be a much more difficult decision to make. The five steps let you build momentum so that, within just a few minutes, you're ready to go instead of feeling groggy.

I have never made it through the first five minutes and decided to go back to bed. Once I am up and moving with intentional through the morning, I can more easily continue being purposeful throughout the day.

Miracle Morning Bonus Wake-Up Tips

Although this strategy has worked for thousands of people, these five steps are not the only way to make waking up in the morning easier. Here are a few others I've heard from fellow Miracle Morning practitioners:

- "The Miracle Morning Bedtime Affirmations": If you haven't done this yet, take a moment now to go to www.TMMbook.com and download the re-energizing, intention-setting "Bedtime Affirmations" for free. Nothing is more effective for ensuring that you will wake up before your alarm than programming your mind to achieve exactly what you want.

- Set a timer for your bedroom lights: One member of the Miracle Morning Community shared that he sets his bedroom lights on a timer (you can buy an appliance timer online or at your local hardware store). As his alarm goes off, the lights come on in the room. What a great idea! It's a lot easier to fall back to sleep when it's dark—having the lights on tells your mind and body that it's time to wake up. Regardless of whether you use a timer, be sure to turn your light on first thing when your alarm goes off.

- Set a timer for your bedroom heater: Another member of the Miracle Morning Community says that in the winter, she keeps a bedroom heater on an appliance timer set to go off fifteen minutes before she wakes up. She keeps it cold at night, but warm for waking up so she won't be tempted to crawl back under her covers.

Feel free to add to or customize the five-step, snooze-proof, wake-up strategy, and if you have any tips that you're open to sharing, we'd love to hear them. Please post them in the Miracle Morning Community at www.MyTMMCommunity.com.

Waking up consistently and easily is all about having an effective, predetermined, step-by-step strategy to increase your WUML in the morning. Don't wait to try this! Start tonight by reading "The Miracle Morning Bedtime Affirmations" to set a powerful intention for waking up tomorrow morning, move your alarm clock across the room, set a glass of water on your nightstand, and commit to the other two steps for the morning.

Taking Immediate Action

There's no need to wait to get started implementing the power of early rising. As Tony Robbins has said, "When is NOW a good time for you to do that?" Now, indeed, would be perfect! In fact, the sooner you start, the sooner you'll begin to see results, including increased energy, a better attitude, and, of course, a happier home life.

Step One: Set your alarm for 30-60 minutes earlier than you usually wake up, for the next 30 days. That's it; just 30-60 minutes for 30 days, starting now. And be sure to write into your schedule to do your first Miracle Morning … *tomorrow morning*. That's right, don't using *waiting until you finish the book* as an excuse to procrastinate on getting started!

If you're feeling resistant at all, because maybe you've tried to make changes in the past but haven't followed through, here's a suggestion: turn now to Chapter 10, The Miracle Morning 30-Day Transformation Challenge, and read ahead. This will give you the mindset and strategy to not only overcome any resistance you may have to getting started, but it will give you the most effective process for implementing a new habit, and sticking with it. Think of it as beginning with the end in mind.

From this day forward, starting with the next 30 days, keep your alarm set for 30–60 minutes earlier than you typically wake up so that you can start waking up when you *want* to, instead of when you *have* to. It's time to start launching each day with a Miracle Morning so that you can become the person you need to be to take yourself and your business to extraordinary levels.

What will you do with that hour? You're going to find out in the next chapter, but for now, simply continue reading this book during your Miracle Morning until you learn the whole routine.

Step Two: Join the Miracle Morning Community at www.MyT-MMCommunity.com to connect with and get support from more than 50,000 like-minded early risers, many of whom have been generating extraordinary results with the Miracle Morning for years.

Step Three: Find a Miracle Morning accountability partner. Enroll someone—your spouse, a friend, family member, coworker, or someone you meet in the Miracle Morning Community—to join you on this adventure so you can encourage, support, and hold each other accountable to follow through until your Miracle Morning has become part of who you are.

Okay, now let's get into the six most powerful, proven, personal development practices known to man (or woman) ... the Life S.A.V.E.R.S.

Entrepreneur Profile

JJ Virgin

JJ Virgin's companies are JJ Virgin & Associates and Mindshare Collaborative.

Top Business Accomplishments

❖ JJ launched her first New York Times best-selling book from the ICU where her son was in a coma from a hit-and-run accident.

❖ She has appeared on Dr. Phil, Dr. Oz, The Doctors, The Today Show, TLC, Food Network, Access Hollywood and Rachel Ray, and has two successful Public Television shows.

❖ She founded and hosts the largest event for health entrepreneurs in the world.

❖ JJ Virgin & Associates has been included on the *Inc. 500* three times, and JJ is a four-time *New York Times* best-selling author.

❖ She is a spokesperson and infomercial host for NutriBullet Lean and has represented Emergen-C, So Delicious Dairy Free, and Subway in the same capacity.

Morning Routine

❖ JJ's Miracle Morning starts the night before. She reviews her agenda for the next day and makes a plan before bed.

❖ She needs eight to nine hours of quality sleep every night, so she gets to bed by 10:00 p.m.

❖ She wakes up around 6:30 a.m. (without an alarm clock). Then she brushes her teeth, drinks coffee (bulletproof coffee beans—black), and takes her morning supplements.

❖ She pulls out her "intentioning journal," where she writes her goals (both short- and long-term) with as much clarity as possible, how she wants the day and week to go, who or what is grateful for, and positive thoughts for both of her sons. She credits this practice for helping her get through her son's accident and hospitalization.

❖ JJ feels most creative in the morning, so this is when she does her brainstorming, creates marketing plans, outlines books and programs, or solves challenges. She explains that this is the most valuable thing she does for her business.

❖ Then she makes her morning shake. She has been drinking protein shakes for breakfast for over 20 years. Her favorite ingredients include protein powder, nut milk, avocado, spinach, and fiber.

❖ Finally, she bathes, dresses, and starts the rest of her day!

— 3 —
THE LIFE S.A.V.E.R.S.
FOR ENTREPRENEURS

Six Practices Guaranteed To Save You
From a Life of Unfulfilled Potential

*What Hal has done with his acronym S.A.V.E.R.S. is take the best practices
—developed over centuries of human consciousness development—and
condensed the "best of the best" into a daily morning ritual.
A ritual that is now part of my day.*

Many people do one *of the S.A.V.E.R.S. daily. For example, many people
do the **E**, they* exercise *every morning. Others do **S** for silence or
meditation, or **S** for* scribing *or journaling. But until Hal packaged
S.A.V.E.R.S., no one was doing all six ancient "best
practices" every morning. The Miracle Morning is perfect for very busy,
successful people. Going through S.A.V.E.R.S. every morning is like
pumping rocket fuel into my body, mind, and spirit ...
before I start my day, every day.*

—ROBERT KIYOSAKI, Best-Selling author of *Rich Dad Poor Dad*

Optimistic. Excited. Successful ... Overwhelmed. Unfulfilled.
Depressed.
    These are just a few of the contradictory words that provide
a fairly accurate description of what it feels like to be an entrepreneur
depending on the day.

Every day, you and I wake up to face the same universal challenge: to overcome our self-imposed limitations and live life to our full potential. Unfortunately, most entrepreneurs never even come close. The large majority settle for far less than they want, wishing they could get to the next level, living with regrets, and never understanding what they need to do to achieve everything they want.

Do you ever feel like that? Like the life and the business you want, and the person you know you need to be to create both, are just beyond your grasp? When you see other entrepreneurs who are excelling in an area, or playing at a level you're not, does it ever seem as if they've got it all figured out? Like they must know something you don't know, because if you knew it, then you'd be excelling too?

Most entrepreneurs live their lives on the wrong side of a significant gap in their potential that separates who they are from who they can become. Often frustrated with themselves and their lack of consistent motivation, effort, and results in one or more areas of life, they spend too much time *thinking* about the actions they should be *taking* to create the results that they want, but then they don't take those actions. More often than not, we know what we need to do... we just don't consistently do what we know.

When Hal experienced the second of his two rock bottoms when his business failed due to the financial collapse of 2008 (the first was when he died for six minutes in a car crash), he felt lost and depressed. He tried to apply what he already knew wasn't working. Nothing he tried was improving his situation. So, he began his own quest for the fastest, most effective strategy to take his success to the next level. He went in search of the best personal development practices that were being practiced by the world's most successful people.

After discovering and assembling a list of six of the most timeless, effective, and proven personal development practices, he first attempted to determine which one or two would accelerate his success the fastest. However, his breakthrough occurred when he asked himself, *what would happen if I did ALL of these?*

So, he did. Within just two months of implementing all six practices, nearly every single day, Hal experienced what you might call miraculous results. He was able to more than double his income, and he went from someone who had never run more than a mile, to training to run a 52-mile ultramarathon—because he *wasn't* a runner and actually despised running. He thought *what better way to take his physical, mental, emotional, and spiritual capacities to another level.* Knowing Hal as well as I do, and spending time with him at several entrepreneurial events, I've seen firsthand the power of his consistently implementing, and mastering, the practices he came to appropriately call the Life S.A.V.E.R.S. I've also watched countless others adopt the S.A.V.E.R.S. and transform themselves, too. I had to follow.

So, whether you're already very successful, like multimillionaire entrepreneur Robert Kiyosaki (who practices the Miracle Morning and the Life S.A.V.E.R.S. almost every day), or if you've ever felt like the life you want to live and the person you know you can be are just beyond your grasp, the Life S.A.V.E.R.S. are virtually guaranteed to save you from missing out on the extraordinary life you truly want.

Why the Life S.A.V.E.R.S. Work

The Life S.A.V.E.R.S. are simple but profoundly effective daily morning practices that are virtually guaranteed to enable you to become more so that you can fulfill your potential. They also give you space to gain heightened levels of clarity to plan and live your life on your terms. They're designed to start your day by putting you in a peak physical, mental, emotional, and spiritual state so you continually improve, will feel great, and *always* perform at your best.

I know, I know. You don't have time. Before starting the Miracle Morning, I would wake up to pure chaos with barely enough time to get dressed and out the door to work. You probably think you can hardly squeeze in what you already have to do, never mind what you want to do. But I "didn't have time" before the Miracle Morning either. And yet, here I am with more time, more prosperity, and a more peaceful life than I've ever had.

What you need to realize right now is that your Miracle Morning will create time for you. The Life S.A.V.E.R.S. are the vehicle to help you reconnect with your true essence and wake up with purpose instead of obligation. The practices help you build energy, see priorities more clearly, and help you find the most productive flow in your life.

In other words, the Life S.A.V.E.R.S. don't take time from your day but ultimately add more to it.

Each letter in the Life S.A.V.E.R.S. represents one of the best practices of the most successful people on the planet. From A-list movie stars and world-class professional athletes to CEOs and entrepreneurs, you'd be hard pressed to find an elite performer that didn't swear by at least one of the S.A.V.E.R.S.

However, you'd be equally hard pressed to find an elite performer that practices even half—let alone *all* the Life S.A.V.E.R.S. (Well, I guess that's changing now that Hal has introduced the world to *The Miracle Morning*.) That's what makes the Miracle Morning so effective; you're harnessing the game-changing benefits of not just one, but all six of *the best practices, developed over centuries of human consciousness development* and combining them into a concise, fully customizable morning ritual.

The Life S.A.V.E.R.S. are:

Silence

Affirmations

Visualization

Exercise

Reading

Scribing

Leveraging these six practices is how you will accelerate your personal development during your newfound Miracle Morning ritual. They're customizable to fit you, your lifestyle, your business, and your specific goals. And you can start implementing them first thing tomorrow morning.

Let's go through each of the Life S.A.V.E.R.S. in detail.

S is for Silence

Silence, the first practice of the Life S.A.V.E.R.S., is a key habit for entrepreneurs. If you've been guilty of starting your day with the endless barrage of emails, phone calls, text messages, meetings, presentations, tracking sheets, and new product launches that make up the life of entrepreneurship, this is your opportunity to begin each day by centering yourself with peaceful, purposeful silence.

Most entrepreneurs start the day by checking email, texts, and the current day's business numbers on their smart phones. And most entrepreneurs struggle to build their businesses. It's not a coincidence. Starting each day with a period of Silence instead will immediately reduce your stress levels and help you begin the day with the kind of calm clarity that you need to focus on what's most important.

Many of the most successful entrepreneurs, and high achievers across all professions, are daily practitioners of silence. It's not surprising that Oprah practices meditation—and that she does nearly all the other Life S.A.V.E.R.S. Musician Katy Perry practices transcendental meditation as do Sheryl Crow and Sir Paul McCartney. Film and television stars Jennifer Aniston, Ellen DeGeneres, Jerry Seinfeld, Howard Stern, Cameron Diaz, Clint Eastwood, and Hugh Jackman have all spoken of their daily meditation practices. Hip-hop mogul Russell Simmons meditates with his two daughters every morning for 20 minutes. Even famous billionaires Ray Dalio and Rupert Murdoch have attributed their financial success to the daily practice of stillness. You'll be in good (and quiet) company by doing the same.

If it seems like I'm asking you to do nothing, let me clarify: you have a number of choices for your practice of silence. In no particular order, here are a few to get you started:

- Meditation
- Prayer
- Reflection
- Deep breathing
- Gratitude

Whichever you choose, be sure you don't stay in bed for your period of silence, and better still, get out of your bedroom altogether.

In an interview with *Shape Magazine*, actress and singer Kristen Bell said, "Do meditative yoga for 10 minutes every morning. When you have a problem—whether it's road rage, your guy, or work—meditation allows everything to unfold the way it's supposed to."

And don't be afraid to expand your horizons. Meditation comes in many forms. As Angelina Jolie told *Stylist Magazine*, "I find meditation in sitting on the floor with the kids coloring for an hour, or going on the trampoline. You do what you love, that makes you happy, and that gives you your meditation."

The Benefits of Silence

How many times, as entrepreneurs, do we find ourselves in stressful situations? How many times are we dealing with immediate obstacles that take us away from our vision or plan? No, those aren't trick questions—the answer is the same for both: every single day. Stress is one of the most common reasons that entrepreneurs lose focus and lose business. Daily, I face the ever-present distractions of other people encroaching on my schedule and the inevitable fires I must extinguish. Quieting the mind allows me to put those things aside and focus on working *on* my business instead of *in* it.

But the effect goes beyond productivity. Excessive stress is terrible for your health too. It triggers your fight-or-flight response, and that releases a cascade of toxic hormones that can stay in your body for days. That's fine if you experience that type of stress only occasionally. But when the constant barrage of seemingly endless tasks you perform as an entrepreneur cause your adrenal glands to flood your body with cortisol, the negative impact on your health adds up.

According to Christopher Bergland, a world-record holding triathlete, coach, and author, "The stress hormone, cortisol, is public health enemy number one. Scientists have known for years that elevated cortisol levels: interfere with learning and memory, lower immune function and bone density, increase weight gain, blood pressure, cholesterol, heart disease ... The list goes on and on.

Chronic stress and elevated cortisol levels also increase risk for depression, mental illness, and lower life expectancy."

Silence in the form of meditation reduces stress, and, as a result, improves your health. A major study run by several groups, including the National Institutes of Health, the American Medical Association, the Mayo Clinic, and scientists from both Harvard and Stanford, revealed that meditation reduces stress and high blood pressure. A recent study by Dr. Norman Rosenthal, a world-renowned psychiatrist who works with the David Lynch Foundation, even found that people who practice meditation are 30 percent less likely to die from heart disease.

Another study from Harvard found that just eight weeks of meditation could lead to "increased gray-matter density in the hippocampus, known to be important for learning and memory, and in structures associated with self-awareness, compassion, and introspection."

Meditation helps you to slow down and focus on you, even if it's for just a short time. Start your meditation practice and say goodbye to feeling scattered and wandering aimlessly without intention and purpose through your day.

"I started meditating because I felt like I needed to stop my life from running me," singer Sheryl Crow has said. "So meditation for me helped slow my day down." She continues to devote 20 minutes in the morning and 20 minutes at night to meditation.

When you are silent, it opens a space for you before you encounter anyone else. The benefits are extraordinary and can bring you much needed clarity and peace of mind so you bring your best self to any interaction. Practicing silence, in other words, can help you reduce your stress, improve cognitive performance, and become confident at the same time.

Guided Meditations and Meditation Apps

Meditation is like anything else, if you've never done it before, it can be difficult or feel awkward at first. If you are a first-time meditator, I recommend starting with a guided meditation.

Here are a few of my favorite meditation apps that are available for both iPhone/iPad and Android devices:

- Headspace
- Calm
- Omvana
- Simply Being
- Insight Timer

There are subtle and significant differences among these meditation apps, one of which is the voice of the person speaking. Experiment and choose what works best for you.

If you don't have a device that allows you to download apps, simply go to YouTube or Google and search for the keywords "Guided Meditation." You can also search by duration (e.g., "five-minute guided meditation") or topic (e.g., "guided meditation for increased confidence").

A cool tool I've been using lately is called Holosync, which uses sound technology to improve meditation. I was blown away at the immediate difference in the depth of my meditation sessions when I started using it. You can try it for free at holosync.com.

Pat Flynn, serial entrepreneur and host of the *Smart Passive Income* podcast, swears by Muse, which is a headband that works in tandem with recordings to enrich your meditation. You can get it at choosemuse.com.

Miracle Morning (Individual) Meditation

When you're ready to try meditating on your own, here is a simple, step-by-step meditation you can use during your Miracle Morning, even if you've never done this before.

- Before beginning, it's important to prepare yourself and set expectations. This is a time for you to quiet your mind and let go of the compulsive need to be thinking about something— reliving the past or worrying about the future, but never living fully in the present. This is the time to let go of your stresses, take a break from worrying about your problems, and be here in this moment. It is a time to access the essence of who you truly are, to go deeper than what you have, what you do, or the labels you've accepted as who you are. If this sounds foreign to you, or too *new agey*, that's okay. I've felt the same way. It's probably because you've never tried it before. But thankfully, you're about to.

- Find a quiet, comfortable place to sit, on the couch, on a chair, on the floor, or on a pillow for added comfort.

- Sit upright, cross-legged. You can close your eyes, or you can look down at a point on the ground about two feet in front of you.

- Begin by focusing on your breath, taking slow, deep breaths. Breathe in through the nose and out through the mouth. The most effective breathing causes your belly to expand and not your chest.

- Now start pacing your breath. Breathe in slowly for a count of three seconds (one one thousand, two one thousand, three one thousand), hold it in for another three counts, and then breathe out slowly for a final count of three. Notice your thoughts and emotions settling down as you focus on your breath. Be aware that, as you attempt to quiet your mind, thoughts will still come in to pay a visit. Simply acknowledge them and let them go, always returning your focus to the breath.

- Allow yourself to be fully present in this moment. Some people refer to this state as *being*. Not thinking, not doing, just being. Continue to follow your breath and imagine inhaling positive, loving, and peaceful energy and exhaling all your worries and stress. Enjoy the quiet. Enjoy the moment. Just breathe … Just be.

- If you find that you have a constant influx of thoughts, it may be helpful for you to focus on a single word, phrase, or mantra to repeat to yourself as you inhale and exhale. For example, you might try something like this: "I inhale confidence …" (on the inhale) "I exhale fear …" (as you exhale). You can swap the word confidence for whatever you feel you need to bring more of into your life (love, faith, energy, strength, etc.), and swap the word fear with whatever you feel you need to let go of (stress, worry, resentment, etc.).

Meditation is a gift you can give yourself every day. My time spent meditating has become one of my favorite parts of the Miracle Morning routine. It's a time to be at peace and to experience gratitude and freedom from my day-to-day stressors and worries.

Think of daily meditation as a temporary vacation from the challenges of life. Although your problems will still be there when you finish each day, you'll find that you're more centered and better equipped to solve them.

A is for Affirmations

Have you ever wondered how some of the top entrepreneurs consistently perform and produce at a level so high, you can hardly comprehend how you're ever going to join them? Or why others in the same business can produce barely enough to scrape by? Time and time again, it is an entrepreneur's *mindset* that shows up as the driving factor in their performance and the underlying cause of their results.

Mindset can be defined as the accumulation of beliefs, attitude, and emotional intelligence. In her best-selling book, *Mindset: The New Psychology of Success*, Carol Dweck, PhD, explains "For twenty years, my research has shown that the view you adopt of yourself profoundly affects the way you lead your life." Show me a great entrepreneur, and I'll show you someone with a great mindset.

Other people around you, from prospective clients to colleagues, can sense your mindset. It shows up undeniably in your language, confidence (or lack thereof), and demeanor. As a result, your mindset affects the entire business building process, from the goals you're willing to consider and the actions you take to your abilities to lead a team and grow your business.

I know firsthand how challenging it can be for entrepreneurs to maintain confidence and enthusiasm—not to mention motivation—during the rollercoaster ride of building their businesses. Mindset is often something we adopt without conscious thought—at a subconscious level, we have all been programmed to think, believe, act, and talk to ourselves a certain way. When times get tough, we revert to our habitual, programmed mindset.

Our programming has come from many sources, including what we have been told by others, what we've told ourselves, and all our good and bad life experiences. That programming expresses itself throughout our lives, including in our businesses. And that means if we want to grow our business, we need to upgrade our mental programming.

Affirmations are a tool for doing just that. They enable you to become more intentional about your goals while also providing the encouragement and positive mindset necessary to achieve them.

Science has proven that affirmations—*when done correctly*—are one of the most effective tools for reprogramming your subconscious mind and quickly becoming the person you need to be to achieve everything you want in your life—for yourself, your business, and your relationships. And yet, affirmations also have a bad rap. Many of us have tried them, only to be disappointed with little or no results. You can, however, leverage affirmations in a way that will absolutely produce results for you. I'll show you how.

By repeatedly articulating and reinforcing to yourself *what* result you want to accomplish, *why* accomplishing it is important to you, *which* specific actions are required to produce that result, and, most importantly, precisely *when* you commit to taking those actions, your subconscious mind will shift your beliefs and behavior. You'll begin to automatically believe and act in new ways and eventually manifest your affirmations into your reality. But first let me explain …

Why the Old Way of Doing Affirmations Doesn't Work

For decades, countless so-called experts and self-help gurus have taught affirmations in ways that have proven to be ineffective and set people up for failure, time and time again. Here are two of the most common problems with affirmations.

Problem #1: Lying to Yourself Doesn't Work

I am a millionaire. Really?

I have 7 percent body fat. Do you?

I have achieved all my goals this year. Have you?

Creating affirmations as if you've already become or achieved something may be the single biggest cause of affirmations not being effective for most people.

With this technique, every time you recite the affirmation that isn't rooted in truth, your subconscious resists it. As an intelligent human being who isn't delusional, lying to yourself repeatedly will never be the optimum strategy. *The truth will always prevail.*

Problem #2: Passive Language Doesn't Produce Results

Many affirmations are designed to make you feel good by creating an empty promise of something you desire. For example, here is a popular money affirmation that's been perpetuated by many:

I am a money magnet. Money flows to me effortlessly and in abundance.

This type of affirmation might make you feel good in the moment by giving you a false sense of relief from your financial worries, but it won't generate any income. People who sit back and wait for money to show up magically are cash poor.

To generate the kind of abundance you want (or any result you desire, for that matter), you've got to actually do something. Your actions must be in alignment with your desired results, and your affirmations must articulate and affirm both.

Four Steps to Create Miracle Morning Affirmations (That Produce Results)

Here are four simple steps for creating and implementing results-oriented Miracle Morning affirmations that will reprogram your subconscious mind and upgrade your mindset while directing your conscious mind to upgrade your behavior so that you produce results and take your levels of personal and entrepreneurial success beyond what you've ever experienced before.

Step One: The Ideal Result You Are Committed to and Why

Notice I'm not starting with what you *want*. Everyone wants things, but we don't get what we want: we get what we're committed to. You want to be a great entrepreneur? You want to be a millionaire? Who among your peers doesn't? Join that nonexclusive club. Oh wait, you're 100 percent committed to becoming a millionaire by clarifying and executing the necessary actions until the result is achieved? Okay, now we're talking.

Action: Start by writing down a specific, extraordinary result or outcome—one that challenges you, would significantly improve your life, and one that you are ready to commit to creating—even if you're not yet sure how you will do it. Then reinforce your commitment by including your *why*, the compelling reason you're willing to stay committed.

Examples: *I am committed to doubling my income in the next 12 months, from $_____ to $_____, so that I can provide financial security for my family.*

Or …

I am 100 percent committed to losing _____ pounds and weighing _____ pounds by _____ (date) so that I have more energy for actions that take my business to the next level.

Step Two: The Necessary Actions You Are Committed to Taking and When

Writing an affirmation that merely affirms what you *want* without affirming what you are committed to *doing* is one step above pointless and can actually be counterproductive by tricking your subconscious mind into thinking that the result will happen automatically and without effort.

Action: Clarify the (specific) action, activity, or habit that is required for you to achieve your ideal outcome, and clearly state when and how often you will execute the necessary action.

Examples: *To ensure that I double my revenue & profit, I am committed to doubling my daily prospecting calls (from 20 to 40 calls) five days a week, between 8:00 a.m. and 9:00 a.m.—NO MATTER WHAT.*

Or …

To ensure that I lose ____ pounds, I am 100 percent committed to going to the gym five days per week and running on the treadmill for a minimum of 20 minutes each day between 6:00 a.m. and 7:00 a.m.

The more specific your actions are, the clearer your programming will be so that you consistently take the actions required to move you closer to your goals. Be sure to include *frequency* (how often), *quantity* (how many), and *precise time frames* (when you will begin and end your activities).

Step Three: Recite Your Affirmations Every Morning with Emotion

Remember, your Miracle Morning affirmations aren't designed only to make you *feel good*. These written statements are strategically engineered to program your subconscious with the mindset you need to achieve your desired outcomes while directing your conscious mind to keep you focused on your highest priorities and taking the actions that will get you there.

For your affirmations to be effective, however, it is important that you tap into your emotions while reciting them. Mindlessly repeating an affirmation without intentionally feeling its truth will have minimal impact for you. You must take responsibility for generating authentic emotions, such as excitement and determination, and powerfully infuse those emotions in every affirmation you recite.

Affirm who you need to be to do the things you need to do so you can have the results you want. I'll say this again: It isn't magic. This strategy works when you connect with *the person you need to become* on the way to achieving your goals. It's who you are that brings about the results more than anything else.

Action: Schedule time each day to read your affirmations during your Miracle Morning to program your subconscious and focus your conscious mind on what's most important to you and what you are committed to doing to make it your reality. That's right, you must read them daily. Reading an occasional affirmation is as effective as getting an occasional workout. You'll start seeing results only when you've made them a part of your daily routine.

A great place to read affirmations is in the shower. If you laminate them and leave them there, then they will be in front of you every day. Put them anywhere you can to remind you: an index card under your car's sun visor, a sticky note on your bathroom mirror. You can even write them directly on a mirror with dry erase markers. The more you encounter them, the more the subconscious mind can connect with them to change your thinking and your actions.

Step Four: Constantly Update and Evolve Your Affirmations

As you continue to grow, improve, and evolve, so should your affirmations. When you come up with a new goal, dream, or any extraordinary result that you want to create for your life, add it to your affirmations.

Personally, I have affirmations for every single significant area of my life (finances, health, happiness, relationships, parenting, etc.) and I continually update them as I learn more. I'm always on the lookout for quotes, strategies, and philosophies that I can add to improve my mindset. Any time you come across an empowering quote or philosophy and think to yourself, *Wow, that is an area where I could make a huge improvement*, add it to your affirmations.

Remember, your affirmations should be tailored to you, what you are *personally* committed to. They must be specific for them to work on *your* subconscious.

Your programming can change and improve at any time, starting right now. You can reprogram any perceived limitations with new beliefs and create new behaviors so you can become as successful as you want to be in any area of life you choose.

In summary, your new affirmations articulate the extraordinary results you are committed to creating, why they are critically important to you, and, most importantly, which necessary actions you are committed to taking and when to ensure that you attain and sustain the extraordinary levels of success you truly want (and deserve) for your life.

Affirmations to Elevate Yourself as an Entrepreneur

In addition to the formula to create your affirmations, I have included this list of sample affirmations, which are regularly used by top entrepreneurs to increase growth and productivity and to improve in different areas of their business. Feel free to include any of these that resonate with you in your daily routine.

- I am just as worthy, deserving, and capable of achieving my ideal outcome as any other person on earth, and I will prove that today with my actions.

- Where I am is a result of who I *was*, but where I go depends entirely on who I *choose to be* starting today.

- I leave every person I speak to better than I found them because I genuinely care about what is happening in their lives, and I'm not afraid to give them an honest compliment. Whether they say yes or no to working with me, they are glad they spoke to me!

- Building my business isn't about me and what I want. It is about connecting with my customers, my prospects, and my team to find out what's important to them and then matching my product or opportunity to meet their wants and needs.

- Remember that people buy products or join companies based on emotion and how they feel, so my job isn't to convince a prospect that they *can't live without* my product or that they must come to work in my business *today*. My intention is to paint a compelling picture (through words and stories) that gets them emotionally engaged in the experience of owning my product and joining my team. I will make it fun and exciting for them to say "yes!"

- One of the true secrets to success as an entrepreneur is to be *committed to my process without being emotionally attached to my results*. I can't always control my daily results, but as long as I follow through with my process that produces those results, the law of averages will *always* play out, and my results will take care of themselves.

- I commit to making a minimum of ___ (number) of (action item), Monday through Friday between ____:____ a.m./p.m. and ____:____ a.m./p.m., no matter what.

- I view my team, customers, and prospects as valued friends, and by focusing on how I can selflessly add value to their lives, I will increase the value I offer them.

- I focus on learning new things and improving my skills daily, and I commit to reading at least one or two new books every month.

- I continue to develop knowledge about my service, and I read industry news weekly to stay ahead of my competition.

- I increase my group volume every month because I am committed to constant and never-ending improvement as well as the action necessary for constant volume growth.

- I dedicate time each week to nurturing my relationships with my customers and team members, and I generate tons of repeat business as a result.

- I am committed to empowering my team with the knowledge and skills that I learn so that they can self-sufficiently attain any level of success that they wish.

These are just a few examples of affirmations. You can use any of these that fell right to you, or create your own affirmations using the four-step formula described in the previous pages. Anything you repeat to yourself over and over again with emotion will be programmed into your subconscious mind, form new beliefs, and manifest itself through your actions.

V is for Visualization

Visualization has long been a well-known practice of world-class athletes who use it to optimize their performance. Olympic athletes and top performers in many sports incorporate visualization as a critical part of their daily training. What is less well known is that the top achievers among successful entrepreneurs use it just as frequently.

Visualization is a technique by which you use your imagination to create a compelling picture of your future, providing you with heightened clarity and producing the motivation that will assist you in making your vision a reality.

To understand *why* visualization works, you need to look at mirror neurons. A neuron is a cell that connects the brain and other parts of the body, and a mirror neuron is one that fires or sends an impulse when we take an action *or* observe someone else taking action. This is a relatively new area of study in neurology, but these cells seem to allow us to improve our abilities by watching other people perform them *or* by visualizing ourselves performing them. Some studies indicate, for example, that experienced weight lifters can increase muscle mass through vivid visualization sessions, and mirror neurons get the credit for making this possible. In many ways, the brain can't tell the difference between a vivid visualization and an actual experience.

I was always a little skeptical about the value of visualization because it sounded a little too new agey. Once I read about mirror neurons, my whole attitude changed!

What Do You Visualize?

Most entrepreneurs are limited by visions of their past results. They replay previous failures and heartbreaks. Creative visualization, however, enables you to *design* the vision that will occupy your mind, ensuring that the greatest pull on you is your future—a compelling, exciting, and limitless future.

Many people don't feel comfortable visualizing success and are even scared to succeed. They may experience resistance to this practice. Some may even feel guilty that they will leave colleagues, friends, and family members behind when they become successful.

This famous quote from, Marianne Williamson, is a great reminder for anyone who feels mental or emotional obstacles when attempting to visualize:

Our deepest fear is not that we are inadequate. Our deepest fear is that we are powerful beyond measure. It is our light, not our darkness that most frightens us. We ask ourselves, "Who am I to be brilliant, gorgeous, talented, fabulous?" Actually, who are you not to be? You are a child of God. Your playing small does not serve the world. There is nothing enlightened about shrinking so that other people won't feel insecure around you. We are all meant to shine, as children do. We were born to make manifest the glory of God that is within us. It's not just in some of us; it's in everyone. And as we let our own light shine, we unconsciously give other people permission to do the same. As we are liberated from our own fear, our presence automatically liberates others.

Consider that the greatest gift you can give to those you love and those you lead is to live to your full potential. What does that look like for you?

After I've read my affirmations during my Miracle Morning practice, I sit upright, close my eyes, and take a few slow, deep breaths. For the next five to ten minutes, I simply visualize the *specific actions* that are necessary for my long- and short-term goals to become a reality.

Notice that I did *not* say that I visualize the results. Many people will disagree on this issue, but there are studies that show that limiting your visualization to a result (the car, the house, crossing the finish line, standing on stage, etc.), can actually diminish your drive, because your brain has already experienced the reward on some level.

Instead, I highly recommend focusing your visualization on the necessary actions. Visualize yourself taking the actions—especially those you habitually resist and procrastinate on—in a way that creates a compelling mental and emotional experience of the action. For example, Hal despised running, but he had made a commitment to himself (and publically) to run a 52-mile ultramarathon. Throughout his five months of training, he used Miracle Morning Visualization to see himself lacing up his running shoes and hitting the pavement—*with a smile on his face and pep in his step*—so that when it was time to train, he had already programmed the experience to be positive and enjoyable.

As an entrepreneur, you might picture yourself having fun and light conversations with prospects during sales calls. Spend time imagining your presentation with your prospect. What does it look like? How does it feel as you develop a great relationship? Picture yourself responding to objections and questions. You can pick anything that is a critical action step or skill that you may not be performing at your best yet. Envisioning success will prepare you for, and almost ensure, a successful day.

Three Simple Steps for Miracle Morning Visualization

The perfect time to visualize yourself living in alignment with your affirmations is right after you read them.

Step One: Get Ready

Some people like to play instrumental music in the background during their visualization, such as classical or baroque (check out anything from the composer J. S. Bach). If you'd like to experiment with music, put it on with the volume relatively low. Personally, I find anything with words to be distracting.

Now, sit up tall in a comfortable position. This can be on a chair, the couch, or the floor with a cushion. Breathe deeply. Close your eyes, clear your mind, and let go of any self-imposed limitations as you prepare yourself for the benefits of visualization.

Step 2: Visualize What You Really Want

What do you really want? Forget about logic, limits, and being practical. If you could reach any heights, personally and professionally, what would that look like? Involve all your senses to maximize effectiveness. See, hear, touch, taste, and smell every detail of your vision. The more vivid you make your vision, the more compelled you'll be to take the necessary actions to make it a reality.

Step 3: Visualize Your Flawless Execution

Once you've created a clear mental picture of what you want, begin to see yourself doing precisely what you need to do to achieve your vision, doing it with supreme confidence, and enjoying every step of the process.

See yourself engaged in the actions you'll need to take (exercising, writing, selling, presenting, public speaking, making calls, sending emails, etc.) Picture yourself with a look and *feeling* of supreme confidence as you pitch that venture capital firm to secure funding. See and *feel* yourself smiling as you're running on that treadmill, filled with a sense of pride for your self-discipline to follow through. In other words, visualize yourself in the midst of *flawless execution*. Feel your determination as you persistently take action and make progress on that project you've been putting off for far too long. Visualize your customers, colleagues, spouse, family, and friends responding to your positive demeanor and optimistic outlook.

Final Thoughts on Visualization

Visualization can be a powerful aid in overcoming self-limiting beliefs, as well as self-limiting habits, such as procrastination, and get you consistently performing the actions necessary to achieve extraordinary results in your business. When you combine reading your affirmations every morning with daily visualization, you will turbocharge the programming of your subconscious mind for success through peak performance. Your thoughts and feelings will align with your vision so that you can maintain the motivation you need to continue to take the necessary actions and achieve your goals and dreams.

E is for Exercise

Exercise should be a staple of your Miracle Morning. Even a few minutes of exercise each day significantly enhances your health, improves your self-confidence and emotional well-being, and enables you to think better and concentrate longer. You'll also notice how quickly your energy increases with daily exercise, and the people you spend the most time with will notice it too.

Personal development experts and self-made multimillionaire entrepreneurs Eben Pagan and Tony Robbins (who is also a best-selling author) both agree that the number one key to success is to start every morning with a personal success ritual. Included in both of their success rituals is some type of morning exercise. Eben is adamant about the importance of *morning* exercise: "Every morning, you've got to get your heart rate up and get your blood flowing and fill your lungs with oxygen." He continued, "Don't just exercise at the end of the day, or at the middle of the day. And even if you do like to exercise at those times, always incorporate at least 10 to 20 minutes of jumping jacks, or some sort of aerobic exercise in the morning." Hey, if it works for Eben and Tony, it works for me!

Lest you think you have to engage in triathlon or marathon training, think again. Your morning exercise also doesn't need to replace an afternoon or evening regimen if you already have one in place. You can still hit the gym at the usual time. However, the benefits from adding as little as five minutes of morning exercise are undeniable, including improved blood pressure and blood sugar levels and decreased risk of all kinds of scary things like heart disease, osteoporosis, cancer, and diabetes. Maybe most importantly, a little exercise in the morning will increase your energy levels for the rest of the day to help you keep up with the ups and downs of life.

You can go for a walk or run, hit the gym, throw on a P90X or Insanity DVD, follow the movements on a yoga video on YouTube, or find a Life S.A.V.E.R.S. buddy to play some early morning racquetball. There's also an excellent app called 7 Minute Workout that gives you a full-body workout in—you guessed it—seven minutes. Those quick workouts are my favorite when I'm on the road doing speaking events because they are easy to fit into my insane schedule. There's no excuse not to do it. The choice is yours— just pick one and do it.

As an entrepreneur, you are on the go. You need an endless reserve of energy to capitalize on all the opportunities coming your way, and a daily morning exercise practice is going to provide it.

Exercise for Your Brain

Even if you don't care about your physical health, consider that exercise is simply going to make you smarter, and that can only help your problem-solving abilities. Dr. Steven Masley, a Florida physician and nutritionist with a health practice geared toward executives, explains how exercise creates a direct connection to your cognitive ability.

"If we're talking about brain performance, the best predictor of brain speed is aerobic capacity—how well you can run up a hill is very strongly correlated with brain speed and cognitive shifting ability," Masley said.

Masley has designed a corporate wellness program based on the work he's done with more than 1,000 patients. "The average person going into these programs will increase brain speed by 25–30 percent."

Hal chose yoga for his exercise activity and began practicing it shortly after he created the Miracle Morning. He's been doing it and loving it ever since. My exercise routine differs.

My exercise routine is usually a run around my neighborhood while listening to great podcasts or audiobooks followed by doing a 7-minute workout. I'm currently training for my first marathon, and I love the sense of peace I get from some time away from my business while running. For me, this accomplishes several things at once: The run helps to wake me up and get my Miracle Morning started, I get a dose of vitamin D for my mind and body, I get a combination of cardio and muscular workout, *and* I get a dose of inspiration from whatever I may be listening to.

My wife works out as part of her Miracle Morning too. Her being active motivates me too! I love that we're both taking action to stay healthy. I encourage you to find what works for you and your life and make it a part of your Miracle Morning.

Final Thoughts on Exercise

You know that if you want to maintain good health and increase your energy, you must exercise consistently. That's not news to anyone. But what also isn't news is how easy it is to make excuses. Two of the biggest are "I don't have time" and "I'm too tired." And those are just the first two on the list. There is no limit to the excuses you can think of. And the more creative you are, the more excuses you can find!

That's the beauty of incorporating exercise into your Miracle Morning—it happens before your day wears you out and before you've had hours to come up with new excuses. Because it comes first, the Miracle Morning is a surefire way to avoid those stumbling blocks and make exercise a daily habit.

Legal disclaimer: Hopefully this goes without saying, but you should consult your doctor or physician before beginning any exercise regimen, especially if you are experiencing any physical pain, discomfort, disabilities, etc. You may need to modify or even refrain from an exercise routine to meet your individual needs.

R is for Reading

As entrepreneurs, we know that one of the fastest ways to achieve the result that we want, is to find successful people to be our role models. For every goal you have, there's a good chance an expert out there has already achieved the same thing or something similar. As Tony Robbins says, "success leaves clues."

Fortunately, some of the best of the best have shared their stories in writing. And that means all those success blueprints are just waiting for anyone willing to invest the time in reading. Books are a limitless supply of help and mentorship right at your fingertips.

One significant challenge for entrepreneurs is that we are driven—even *addicted*—to producing results. It's our blessing and our curse. It's a blessing because it's what sets you apart from the majority of our society who are content clocking in and out, and putting forth minimal effort for moderate compensation. It's what gives you the drive to create, add value, and make an impact in the world.

This addiction to producing results is also a curse because too often it prevents us from dedicating time to work on improving ourselves and our businesses. Since reading doesn't *directly* produce results (at least not in the short term), our natural entrepreneurial gene, if there is such a thing, pulls us into other activities that more obviously bear fruit. The problem is that those results are often low-level tasks, such as checking email.

Occasionally, I hear an entrepreneur say, "I'm so busy I don't have time to read." I get it. I used to have that belief as well. But now I think of what my mentor used to say: "The greatest minds in human history have spent years condensing the best of what they know into a few pages that can be purchased for a few dollars, read in a few hours, and shorten your learning curve by decades. But I get it ... you're too busy." Ouch!

Want to go from zero to $100 million in no time flat? Want to learn how to think and grow rich? Ready to awaken the giant within? Be happy for no reason? Implement a four-hour workweek? Double your revenue and profit in three years or less? You're in luck ... I've heard that several authors have written books on precisely those topics.

As for some of my favorite books related to entrepreneurship, here's a short list:

- *Scale: Seven Proven Principles to Grow Your Business and Get Your Life Back* by Jeff Hoffman and David Finkel

- *Getting Everything You Can Out of All You've Got: 21 Ways You Can Out-Think, Out-Perform, and Out-Earn the Competition* by Jay Abraham

- *Zero to One: Notes on Startups, or How to Build the Future* by Peter Thiel

- *The Lean Startup: How Today's Entrepreneurs Use Continuous Innovation to Create Radically Successful Businesses* by Eric Ries

- *Ask: The Counterintuitive Online Method to Discover Exactly What Your Customers Want to Buy ... Create a Mass of Raving Fans ... and Take Any Business to the Next Level* by Ryan Levesque

- *The One Thing: The Surprisingly Simple Truth Behind Extraordinary Results* by Gary Keller and Jay Papasan

- *Ego Is the Enemy* by Ryan Holiday

- *Influence: The Psychology of Persuasion* by Robert Cialdini

Here are several additional titles on mindset:

- *The Art of Exceptional Living* by Jim Rohn

- *Think and Grow Rich* by Napoleon Hill

- *The Power of Consistency: Prosperity Mindset Training for Sales and Business Professionals* by Weldon Long

- *The 7 Habits of Highly Effective People: Powerful Lessons in Personal Change* by Stephen R. Covey

- *Mastery* by Robert Greene

- *The 4 Hour Workweek: Escape 9–5, Live Anywhere, and Join the New Rich* by Tim Ferriss

- *The Game of Life and How to Play It* by Florence Scovel Shinn

- *The Compound Effect* by Darren Hardy

- *Taking Life Head On: How to Love the Life You Have While You Create the Life of Your Dreams* by Hal Elrod

- *Vision to Reality: How Short Term Massive Action Equals Long Term Maximum Results* by Honorée Corder

- *Finding Your Element: How to Discover Your Talents and Passions and Transform Your Life* by Sir Ken Robinson and Lou Aronica

In addition to finding success as an entrepreneur, you can transform your relationships, increase your self-confidence, improve your communication or persuasion skills, learn how to become healthy, and improve any other area of your life you can imagine.

For a complete list of Hal's favorite personal development books—including those that have made the biggest impact on his success, health, and happiness—check out the *Recommended Reading* list at TMMBook.com.

How Much Should You Read?

I recommend making a commitment to read a minimum of ten pages per day (although five is okay to start with if you read slowly or don't yet enjoy reading).

Ten pages may not seem like a lot, but let's do the math. Reading ten pages a day adds up to 3,650 pages per year, which stacks up to approximately eighteen 200-page books that will enable you to take yourself to the next level so that you can take your success in your business to the next level—all in just 10–15 minutes of daily reading or 15–30 minutes if you read more slowly.

Let me ask you, if you read 18 personal and professional development books in the next twelve months, do you think you'll improve your mindset, gain more confidence, and learn proven strategies that will accelerate your success? Do you think you'll be a better, more capable version of who you are today? Do you think that will be reflected in your business? Absolutely! Reading ten pages per day is not going to break you, but it will absolutely make you.

Final Thoughts on Reading

- Begin with the end in mind by considering this question: What do you hope to gain from the book? Take a moment to do this now by asking yourself what you want to gain from reading this one.

- Books don't have to be read cover to cover, nor do they have to be finished. Remember that this is *your* reading time. Use the table of contents to make sure you read the parts you care about most, and don't hesitate to put it down and move to another book if you aren't enjoying it or gaining value from it. You have too many options for incredible information to spend time on the mediocre. In fact, I suggest you read my first book, *Double Double*, and be sure to read only the chapters you feel apply best to you.

- Unless you're borrowing a book from the library or a friend, feel free to underline, circle, highlight, dog-ear, and take notes in the margins of the book. The process of marking books as you read allows you to come back at any time and recapture the key lessons, ideas, and benefits without needing to read the book again. If you use a digital reader, such as Kindle, Nook, or an iBooks app, notes and highlighting are easily organized, so you can see them each time you flip through the book, or you can go directly to a list of your notes and highlights.

- Summarize key ideas, insights, and memorable passages in a journal. You can build your own summary of your favorite books so you can revisit the key content anytime in just minutes.

- Rereading good personal development books is an underused yet very effective strategy. Rarely can you read a book once and internalize all its value. Achieving mastery in any area requires repetition. I've read books like *Think and Grow Rich* as many as three times and often refer back to them throughout the year. Why not try it out with this book? Commit to rereading *The Miracle Morning for Entrepreneurs* as soon as you're finished to deepen your learning and give yourself more time to master the practices.

- Audiobooks count as reading! You still get the information, and you can do it while exercising or during your commute. If you want to study a book closely, listen to the audio while reading the text. As I mentioned earlier, I enjoy listening to audiobooks while I run. I'm able to accomplish two things at once, and the excitement I feel for the inspirational material I listen to influences how I feel about my workout, and vice versa.

- Most importantly, quickly implement what you read. Schedule time to implement action steps based on advice you want to implement *while you're reading it.* Keep your calendar next to you and schedule time blocks to put the content into action. Don't become a personal development junkie who reads a lot but does very little. I've met many people who take pride in the number of books they read, as if it's some badge of honor. I'd rather read and implement one good book than read 10 books and do nothing other than start reading the 11th book. While reading is a great way to gain knowledge, insights, and strategies, it is the application and practice of what you learn that will advance life and business. Are you committed to using what you're learning in this book by taking action and following through with the 30-Day Challenge at the end?

Glad to hear it! Let's get to the final *S* of the Life S.A.V.E.R.S.

S is for Scribing

Scribing is simply another word for writing. Let's keep it real—Hal needed an *S* for the end of Life S.A.V.E.R.S. because the *W* wouldn't fit anywhere. Thanks thesaurus, we owe you one.

Most Miracle Morning practitioners scribe in a journal, for five to ten minutes, during their Miracle Morning. By getting your thoughts out of your head and putting them in writing, you'll immediately gain heightened awareness, clarity, and valuable insights that you'd otherwise be oblivious to. The scribing element of your Miracle Morning enables you to write down what you're grateful for, as well as document your insights, ideas, breakthroughs, realizations, successes, and lessons learned, including any areas of opportunity, personal growth, or improvement.

If you're like Hal used to be, you probably have at least a few half-used and barely touched journals and notebooks. It wasn't until he started his Miracle Morning practice that scribing quickly became one of his favorite daily habits.

Writing will give you the daily benefits of consciously direct-ing your thoughts, but what's even more powerful are the insights you'll gain from reviewing your journals, from cover to cover, afterwards—especially at the end of the year. As Tony Robbins has said many times, "A life worth living is a life worth recording."

It is hard to put into words how overwhelmingly constructive the experience of going back and reviewing your journals can be. Michael Maher, *The Miracle Morning for Real Estate Agents* co-author, is an avid practitioner of the Life S.A.V.E.R.S. Part of Michael's morning routine is to record his appreciations and affirmations in what he calls his Blessings Book. Michael says it best:

"What you appreciate ... APPRECIATES. It is time to take our insatiable appetite for what we want and replace it with an insatiable appetite and gratitude for what we do have. Write your ap-preciations, be grateful and appreciative, and you will have more of those things you crave—better relationships, more material goods, more happiness."

A great practice to add to your routine is to write what you appreciate about different aspects of your business. When we write down the things we appreciate about our team and their performance, for example, even (and particularly) when we feel less than wonderful about it, it's easier to focus and capitalize on what's going well. The practice of recording appreciations helps you focus on the positive, which will help you stay flexible and solution focused even when circumstances are challenging.

While many worthwhile benefits flow from keeping a daily journal, here are a few of my favorites. With daily scribing, you'll

- **Gain Clarity**—Journaling will give you more clarity and understanding of your past and current circumstances, help you work through present challenges you're facing, and allow you to brainstorm, prioritize, and plan your actions each day to optimize your future.

- **Capture Ideas**—You will be able to capture, organize, and expand on your ideas and keep from losing the important ones you are saving for an opportune moment in the future.

- **Review Lessons**—Journaling provides a place to record, reference and review all the lessons you're learning, both from your wins and any mistakes you make along the way.

- **Acknowledge Your Progress**—Rereading your journal entries from a year or even a week ago and observing how much progress you've made can be hugely beneficial. We often accomplish a task or goal and move on to the next without appreciating our efforts. Noticing how far you've come truly is one of the most enjoyable, eye-opening, and confidence-inspiring experiences, and it can't be duplicated any other way.

- **Improve Your Memory**—People tend to assume they will remember things, but if you've ever gone to the grocery store without a list, you know this is simply untrue. When we write something down, we are much more likely to remember it, and if we forget, we can always go back and read it again.

Gap Focus: Is It Hurting or Helping You?

The gap in human potential varies in size from person to person. You may feel as if you're very near your current potential and that a few tweaks could make all the difference. Or you might feel the opposite—your potential is so far away from who you've been that you don't even know where to start. Whatever the case is for you, know that it is absolutely possible and attainable for you to live your life on the right side of your potential gap and become the person you are capable of becoming.

Whether you are currently sitting on the wrong side of a grand-canyon-sized gap in your potential, and feeling like you're never going to get to the other side, or you've been working your way across the canyon but are stuck at a particular point and haven't been able to close that gap, it's time to shift your focus.

Human beings have been conditioned to habitually operate from a place of *gap focus.* We tend to notice the gaps between where we are and where we want to be: between what we've accomplished and what we could have, should have, or want to have accomplished. And we concentrate on the gap between who we are and our idealistic, perfect vision of the person we believe we should be.

The problem is that our constant gap focus can be detrimental to our confidence and self-image, causing us to feel like we don't have enough, haven't accomplished enough, and that we're simply not good enough, or at least, not as good as we should be. *And never will be.*

High achieving entrepreneurs are typically the worst at this, constantly overlooking or minimizing their accomplishments, beating themselves up over every mistake and imperfection, ending every day knowing they could have done more, and never feeling like anything they do is quite good enough.

The irony is that gap focus is a big part of the reason why high achievers achieve all that they do. Their insatiable desire to close the gap is what fuels their pursuit of excellence and constantly drives them to achieve. Gap focus can be healthy and productive if it comes from a positive, proactive perspective without feelings of lack: "I'm committed to and excited about fulfilling my potential." Unfortunately, it rarely does. The average person, even the average high achiever, tends to focus negatively on their gaps.

The *highest* achievers—those who are balanced and who focus on elevating themselves to level 10 in nearly every area of their lives—are exceedingly grateful for what they have, regularly acknowledge themselves for what they've accomplished, and are always at peace with where they are in their lives. It's holding the paradox that *I am doing the best that I can in this moment,* and at the same time, *I can and will do better.* This balanced self-assessment prevents that feeling of lack—of not being, having, or doing enough—while still allowing them to constantly strive to close their potential gap in each area.

Typically, when a day, week, month, or year ends, and we're in gap focus mode, it's almost impossible to maintain an accurate assessment of ourselves and our progress. For example, if you had 10 things on your to-do list for the day—even if you completed six of them—your gap focus causes you to feel you didn't get everything done that you intended to do.

The majority of people do dozens, even hundreds, of things *right* during the day and a few things wrong. Guess which things people remember and replay in their minds over and over again? Doesn't it make more sense to focus on the 100 things you did right? It sure is more enjoyable.

What does this have to do with scribing? Scribing, specifically writing in a journal each day, with a structured, strategic process (more on that in a minute) allows you to direct your focus to what you *did* accomplish, what you *are* grateful for, and what you're committed to doing better today. This practice enables you to more deeply enjoy your journey each day, feel good about the forward progress you made, and use a heightened level of clarity to accelerate your results.

While scribing will give you the immediate, daily benefits of consciously directing your thoughts and focus, what can be even more powerful are the insights you'll gain from reviewing and rereading your journals, afterward. It is hard to put into words how constructive the experience of going back and reviewing your journals can be.

Effective Journaling

Here are three simple steps to get started with journaling or improve your current process.

Step One. Choose a format. physical or digital. You'll want to decide up front if you prefer a traditional, physical journal or a digital journal (on your computer or an app for your mobile device). If you aren't sure, experiment with both and see which feels best.

Step Two. Obtain the journal of your choice. Almost anything can work, but when it comes to a physical journal, there is something to be said for a durable one that you enjoy looking at—after all, ideally you're going to have it for the rest of your life. I like to buy high quality leather journals with lines on the pages, but it's your journal, so choose what works best for you. Some people prefer journals without lines so they can draw or create mind maps. Others like to have a predated book with a page for each day of the year to help them stay accountable.

Here are a few favorite physical journals from TMM Facebook Community:

- *The Five Minute Journal* has become popular among top performers. It has a very specific format for each day with prompts, such as "I am grateful for …" and "What would make today great?" It takes five minutes or less and includes an evening option so you can review your day. (FiveMinuteJournal.com)

- *The Freedom Journal* gives you a structured daily process that is focused on helping you with a single objective: *Accomplish Your #1 Goal in 100 Days*. Beautifully designed by John Lee Dumas of Entrepreneur On Fire, it's designed specifically to help you set and accomplish one big goal at a time. (TheFreedomJournal.com)

- *The Bullet Journal* (BulletJournal.com) is a journal you can buy, but it's also a customizable journaling system that you can incorporate into the physical journal of your choice. It can be your to-do list, sketchbook, notebook, and diary, but most likely, it will be all of the above. Our co-author, Honorée swears by her Bullet Journal, using it as her daily organization system.

- *The Miracle Morning Journal* is designed specifically to enhance and support your Miracle Morning and to keep you organized and accountable and to track your Life S.A.V.E.R.S. each day. You can also download a free sample of *The Miracle Morning Journal* today at TMMbook.com to make sure it's right for you. (MiracleMorningJournal.com)

If you prefer to use a digital journal, there are also many choices available. Here are a few of our favorites:

- *Five Minute Journal* also offers an iPhone app, which follows the same format as the physical version, but allows you to upload photographs to your daily entries, and sends you helpful reminders to input your entries each morning and evening. (FiveMinuteJournal.com)

- *Day One* is a popular journaling app, and it's perfect if you don't want any structure or any limits on how much you can write. Day One offers a blank page for each daily entry, so if you like to write lengthy journal entries, this may be the app for you. (DayOneApp.com)

- *Penzu* is a popular online journal, which doesn't require an iPhone, iPad, or Android device. All you need is a computer. (Penzu.com)

Again, it really comes down to your preference and the features you want. If none of these digital options resonate with you, type "online journal" into Google, or simply type "journal" into the app store, and you'll get a variety of choices.

Step Three. Scribe daily. There are endless things you can write about—notes from the book you're reading, a list of things you're grateful for, and your top 3-5 priorities for the day are a good place to start. Write whatever makes you feel good and optimizes your day. Don't worry about grammar, spelling, or punctuation. Your journal is a place to let your imagination run wild; so keep a muzzle on your inner critic and don't edit—just scribe!

Customizing Your Life S.A.V.E.R.S.

I know that you might have days when you can't do the Miracle Morning practice all at once. Feel free to split up the Life S.A.V.E.R.S.

I want to share a few ideas specifically geared toward customizing the Life S.A.V.E.R.S. based on your schedule and preferences. Your current morning routine might allow you to fit in only a 6-, 20-, or 30-minute Miracle Morning, or you might choose to do a longer version on the weekends.

Here is an example of a fairly common 60-minute Miracle Morning schedule.

Silence: 10 minutes

Affirmations: 10 minutes

Visualization: 5 minutes

Exercise: 10 minutes

Reading: 20 minutes

Scribing: 5 minutes

You can customize the sequence, too. I prefer to do my exercise first as a way to increase my blood flow and wake myself up. However, you might prefer to do exercise as your last activity so you're not sweaty during your Miracle Morning. Hal prefers to start with a period of peaceful, purposeful Silence so that he can wake up slowly, clear his mind, and focus his energy and intentions. However, this is your Miracle Morning, not ours—feel free to experiment with different sequences to see which you like best.

Ego Depletion and Your Miracle Morning

Have you ever wondered why you can resist sugary snacks in the morning, but your resistance crumbles in the afternoon or evening? Why is it that sometimes willpower is strong and other times it deserts us? It turns out that willpower is like a muscle that grows tired from use, and at the end of the day, it is harder to push ourselves to do activities that serve us and avoid those that don't.

The good news is that we know how this works and can set ourselves up for success with some advanced planning. And the great news? The Miracle Morning is an integral part of your plan. To see how this works, we need to understand ego depletion.

Ego depletion is a term to describe "a person's diminished capacity to regulate their thoughts, feelings, and actions," according to Roy F. Baumeister and John Tierney, the authors of *Willpower: Rediscovering the Greatest Human Strength*. Ego depletion grows worse at the end of the day and when we are hungry, tired, or have had to exert our willpower too often or for long durations.

If you wait until the end of the day to do important things that give you energy and help you become the person and entrepreneur you want to be, you'll find that your excuses are more compelling and your motivation has gone missing. But, when you wake up and do your Miracle Morning first thing, you gain the increased energy and mindfulness that the Life S.A.V.E.R.S. provide and keep ego depletion from getting in your way.

When you perform the Life S.A.V.E.R.S. habit every day, you learn the mechanics of habit formation when your willpower is strongest, and you can use this knowledge and energy to adopt small and doable habits at other times of the day.

Final Thoughts on the Life S.A.V.E.R.S.

Everything is difficult before it's easy. Every new experience is uncomfortable before it's comfortable. The more you practice the Life S.A.V.E.R.S., the more natural and normal each of them will feel.

Hal's first time meditating was almost his last because his mind raced like a Ferrari, and his thoughts bounced around uncontrollably like the silver sphere in a pinball machine. Now, he loves meditation, and while he's still no master, he says he's decent at it.

Similarly, I had trouble with affirmations when I first started my Miracle Mornings. I didn't know what I wanted to affirm. I used a few from *The Miracle Morning* and added a few that came to mind. It was okay, but they didn't really *mean* much to me initially. Over time, as I encountered things that struck me as powerful, I added them to my affirmations and adjusted the ones I had. Now, my affirmations mean a lot to me, and the daily act of using them is far more powerful.

I invite you to begin practicing the Life S.A.V.E.R.S. now, so you can become familiar and comfortable with each of them and get a jump-start before you begin the Miracle Morning 30-Day Life Transformation Challenge in chapter 10.

The Six-Minute Miracle Morning

If your biggest concern is finding time, don't worry. I've got you covered. You can actually do the entire Miracle Morning—receiving the full benefits of all six Life S.A.V.E.R.S.—in only six minutes a day. While six minutes isn't the duration I'd recommend on a daily basis, for those days when you're pressed for time, simply do each of the Life S.A.V.E.R.S. for one minute each:

Minute One (S): Close your eyes and enjoy a moment of peaceful, purposeful silence to clear your mind and get centered for your day.

Minute Two (A): Read your most important affirmation to reinforce *what* result you want to accomplish, *why* it's important to you, *which* specific actions you must take, and, most importantly, precisely *when* you will commit to taking those actions

Minute Three (V): Visualize yourself flawlessly executing the single most important action that you want to mentally rehearse for the day.

Minute Four (E): Stand up and engage in some high energy jumping jacks or drop and do push-ups and crunches, to get your heart rate up and engage your body.

Minute Five (R): Grab the book you're reading and read a page or paragraph.

Minute Six (S): Grab your journal and jot down one thing that you're grateful for and the single most important result for you to generate that day.

I'm sure you can see how, even in just six minutes, the S.A.V.E.R.S. will serve to set you on the right path for the day—and you can always devote more time later in the day when your schedule permits or the opportunity presents itself. Doing the six-minute practice is a great way to start a mini habit to build your confidence or a way to book-mark the habit on a tough morning. Another mini habit you could do is to start with one of the Life S.A.V.E.R.S., and once you get used to waking up earlier, add more of them. Remember that the goal is to have some time to work on your personal goals and mindset, so if you are overwhelmed, it's not going to work for you.

Personally, my Miracle Morning has grown into a daily ritual of renewal and inspiration that I absolutely love! In the coming chapters, I will build on the benefits of the Life S.A.V.E.R.S. and cover *a lot* of information that has the potential to turn you into a truly confident entrepreneur. I can't wait to share it with you.

Entrepreneur Profile

Yanik Silver

Yanik Silver's company is EvolvedEnterprise.com.

Top Business Accomplishments

❖ Yanik's first million-dollar idea came to him in the morning, at 3:00 a.m. to be exact.

❖ He bootstrapped seven products and services from scratch to hit the 7-figure mark without funding, taking on debt, or having a real business plan.

❖ He believes in giving back, and his companies have contributed more than $3.5 million to entrepreneurial causes and nonprofit partners.

❖ Yanik has run programs with icons such as Sir Richard Branson, Tony Hawk, Chris Blackwell, John Paul DeJoria, Tony Hsieh, Russell Simmons, and Tim Ferriss.

❖ He was asked to serve on the board of Virgin Unite, Richard Branson's nonprofit.

Morning Routine

❖ Yanik's morning starts at around 8:30 a.m.

❖ He drinks eight ounces of water with freshly squeezed lemon.

❖ He does yoga for 30 minutes on his back deck.

❖ Then he meditates for 20 minutes.

❖ Yanik journals for 10–15 minutes, focusing on gratitude or thoughts that have come up during his meditation.

❖ He enjoys music while eating his breakfast.

❖ He takes local honey, bee pollen, and other supplements.

❖ Then he reads for 15–30 minutes, typically something inspirational or about the "big picture" of cosmology.

❖ He checks his email then writes, creates content, or holds meetings.

SECTION 2:

THE ENTREPRENEUR'S ELEVATION SKILLS

— 4 —

Entrepreneur Elevation Skill #1:

SELF-LEADERSHIP

Your level of success will seldom exceed your level of personal development, because success is something you attract by the person that you become.
—JIM ROHN

We've been lied to. Yep. Society has conditioned all of us to think that the only way to have more is to do more.

Want more money? Work harder. Put in *more* hours.

Want more sex? Lift *more* weights and log *more* steps on your fitness tracker.

Want more love? Do *more* for your partner than they do for you.

But what if the real secret to having more of what we want in our lives is not about *doing* more, but it's really about *becoming* more.

It is this philosophy that gave birth to, and remains the foundation of, the Miracle Morning: Our level of success *in every single area of our lives* is always determined by our levels of *personal development* (i.e., our beliefs, knowledge, emotional intelligence, skills, abilities, faith, etc.). So if we want to have more, we must first become more.

Think of it this way: If you were to measure your desired level of success on a scale of one to ten in every area of your life, it's safe to say that you want level 10 success in each area. I've never met anyone who said, "Nah, I don't want to be too happy, too healthy, or too wealthy. I am content settling for less than my potential and cruising along with a level 5 life."

So the question is, what are you going to do each day to ensure that you become a level 10 person so that level 10 success is virtually guaranteed for you?

In other words, who you're becoming is far more important than what you're doing, and yet the irony is that what you're doing, each day is determining who you're becoming.

Hopefully, by now, you've started the Miracle Morning and are beginning your days with the Life S.A.V.E.R.S., or at least a few of them. The distinction here is that who you're becoming is far more important than what you're doing. Yet the irony is that what you're doing, each day, is determining who you're becoming.

As a fellow entrepreneur, I know that you know how hard (read: impossible) it is to sell others on something if you aren't sold on it yourself.

Your role as an entrepreneur is to find people who can benefit from the products and services you offer. If you don't believe your business or products are highly beneficial for the customer, it's impossible to convince others to purchase from you. You also have to build a team of people who believe in what you offer, like you do, to help you grow your business.

You lead your prospective customers to make the best buying decisions for them by guiding them through all their options. And just as it's impossible to sell something if you don't believe in it yourself, it's impossible to lead others if you don't know how to effectively lead yourself.

Andrew Bryant, founder of Self-Leadership International, summed it up this way: "Self-leadership is the practice of intentionally influencing your thinking, feeling, and behaviors to achieve your objective(s) ... [It] is having a developed sense of who you are, what you can do, and where you are going coupled with the ability to influence your communication, emotions, and behaviors on the way to getting there."

Before I reveal the key principles of self-leadership, I want to share with you what I've discovered about the crucial role that *mindset* plays as the foundation of effective self-leadership. Your past beliefs, self-image, and the ability to collaborate with and rely upon others at critical times will factor into your ability to excel as a self-leader.

Be Aware and Skeptical of Your Self-Imposed Limitations

You may be holding on to false limiting beliefs that are unconsciously interfering with your ability to achieve your business goals.

For example, you may be someone who repeats "I wish I was more motivated" or "I wish I were better at finding great people." Yet in reality you are more than capable of generating motivation and filling your calendar with appointments. Thinking of yourself as less than capable assumes imminent failure and simultaneously thwarts your ability to succeed. Life contains enough obstacles without creating more for yourself!

Effective self-leaders closely examine their beliefs, decide which ones serve them, and eliminate the ones that don't.

When you find yourself thinking or saying anything that sounds like a limiting belief, from "I don't have enough time" to "I could never do that," pause and turn your self-limiting statements into empowering questions: *Where can I find more time in my schedule? How could I do that?*

Doing this allows you to tap into your inborn creativity and find a way to make anything happen. There's always a way when you're committed.

See Yourself as Better than You've Ever Been

As Hal wrote in *The Miracle Morning*, most of us suffer from Rearview Mirror Syndrome, limiting our current and future results based on who we were in the past. Remember that, although *where you are is a result of who you were, where you go depends entirely on the person you choose to be from this moment forward.* This is especially important for us as entrepreneurs. We will make mistakes. But don't let your sense of guilt about that keep you from looking forward. Learn from your mistakes and do better next time.

All successful entrepreneurs—especially the top 1 percent—at some point made the choice to see themselves as better than they had ever been before. They stopped maintaining limiting beliefs based on their past and instead started forming their beliefs based on their unlimited potential.

One of the best ways to do this is to follow the four-step Miracle Morning Affirmations formula for creating results-oriented affirmations outlined in the last chapter. Be sure to create affirmations that reinforce what's possible for you by reminding you of the ideal outcome, why it's important to you, which actions you're committed to taking to achieve it, and precisely when you're committed to taking those actions.

Actively Seek Support

I've coached hundreds of entrepreneurs on how to grow their companies, come to grips with their innate talents and abilities as well as challenges and weaknesses, and engage the support they need. Those who struggle the most are the ones who suffer in silence. They assume everyone else has greater capabilities, and they all but refuse to seek help and assistance.

If that describes you, then this might help: Every entrepreneur I've met each has a team that supports them. They know what they excel at and where they fall short. Not only have they embraced the gaps and found solutions, they are just fine with their humanity.

Entrepreneurs who are self-leaders know they need a team to provide the support to get things done. You might need administrative support, for example, so you can do what you do best: grow your business! You may need accountability support to overcome your tendency to procrastinate. We all need support in different areas of our lives, and great self-leaders understand that and use it to their benefit.

The Miracle Morning Community on Facebook is a great place to start looking for support. The members are positive and responsive. You could also try joining a local group for people with similar business goals and interests. I highly recommend getting an accountability partner and, if you can, a life or business coach to help you.

The Five Foundational Principles of Self-Leadership

Self-leadership is a skill, and all skills are built on a foundation of principles. To grow and reach the levels of success you aspire to reach, you'll need to become a proficient self-leader. My favorite way to cut the learning curve in half and decrease the time it takes to reach the top 1 percent is to adapt the principles, traits, and behaviors of those who have come before me to my circumstances. During my twenty-five years coaching entrepreneurs, I've seen many leaders and a myriad of effective strategies. Here are the five principles I believe will make the biggest impact on your commitment to self-leadership:

1. Take 100 Percent Responsibility
2. Prioritize Fitness and Make Exercise Enjoyable
3. Aim for Financial Freedom
4. Systematize Your World
5. Commit to Your Result-Producing Process

Principle #1: Take 100 Percent Responsibility

Here's the hard truth: If your life and business are not where you want them to be, it's all on you.

The sooner you take ownership of that fact, the sooner you'll begin to move forward. This isn't meant to be harsh. Successful people are rarely victims. In fact, one of the reasons they are successful is that they take absolute, total, and complete responsibility for each and every aspect of their lives—whether it's personal or professional, good or bad, their job or someone else's.

While victims habitually waste their time and energy blaming others and complaining, achievers are busy creating the results and circumstances they want for their lives. While mediocre entrepreneurs complain that their prospects aren't buying for *this* or *that* reason, or that it's their team's fault for underperforming, successful entrepreneurs have taken 100 percent responsibility for finding the right prospects and, more importantly, acquiring the skills necessary to build volume and get people started correctly. They're so busy working that they don't have time to complain.

I heard Hal articulate a profound distinction during one of his keynote speeches: "The moment you take 100 percent responsibility for everything in your life is the same moment you claim your power to change anything in your life. However, the crucial distinction is to realize that taking responsibility is not the same thing as accepting *blame*. While blame determines who is at fault for something, responsibility determines who is committed to improving a situation. It rarely matters who is at fault. All that matters is that *you* are committed to improving your situation." He's right. And it's so empowering when you truly start to think and act accordingly. Suddenly, your life, and your results, are within your control.

When you take true ownership of your life, there's no time to discuss whose fault something is or who gets the blame. Playing the blame game is easy, but there's no longer any place for it in your life. Finding reasons for why you didn't meet your goals is for the other guy, not you. You own your results—good and bad. You can celebrate the good and learn from the so-called bad. Either way, you always have a choice about how you respond or react in any and every situation.

One of the reasons this mindset is so important is that you are leading by example. If you're always looking for someone to the blame, your team sees that, and they likely don't respect it. Like a parent trying to bring out the best in their kids, the people you lead are always watching you, and it's crucial to live by the values that you want to instill in each of them.

Here's the psychological shift I suggest you make: Take owner-ship and stewardship over all your decisions, actions, and outcomes, starting right now. Replace unnecessary blame with unwavering responsibility. Even if someone else drops that ball, ask yourself what you could have done, and, more importantly, what you can do in the future to prevent that ball from being dropped. While you can't change what's in the past, the good news is that you can change everything else.

From now on, there's no doubt about who is at the wheel and who is responsible for all your results. You make the calls, do the follow up, decide the outcomes you want, and you get them. Your results are 100 percent your responsibility. Right?

Remember you are in the position of power, you are in control, and there are no limits to what you can accomplish.

Where is Your Self-Discipline?

Self-discipline is the ability to make yourself do the things that you know are in your long-term best interest. In many cases, it is simply the ability to resist short-term temptation. When used wisely and with common sense, self-discipline becomes one of the most important tools for self-improvement and entrepreneurial success.

Self-discipline is helpful when addressing addictions or any kind of incongruous behavior. It will improve your relationships, help you develop patience and tolerance, and is important for attaining success and happiness. Imagine having the self-discipline to handle anything that comes your way.

How does self-discipline help you? Let me count the ways ...

- Keeps in check self-destructive, addictive, obsessive, and compulsive behavior.
- Gives you a sense of mastery and balance in your life.
- Helps to keep inappropriate emotional responses in check.
- Eliminates feelings of helplessness and dependency on others.

- Helps to manifest mental and emotional detachment (really important as an entrepreneur), which contributes to peace of mind.
- Enables you to control your moods and reject negative feelings and thoughts.
- Strengthens self-esteem, confidence, inner strength, self-mastery, and willpower.
- Enables you to take charge of your life.
- Makes you an emotionally stable human being.

How to Develop Self-Discipline

1. First, you need to identify the areas of your life where you need to gain more self-discipline. Where do you find yourself lacking?

Possible areas could be

- Eating
- Spending
- Drinking
- Working
- Gambling
- Smoking
- Obsessive behavior
- Procrastinating
- Loving (yes, love requires discipline in the long term)

2. Try to identify the emotions that indicate a lack of control, such as anger, dissatisfaction, unhappiness, resentment, pleasure, or fear.

3. Identify the thoughts and beliefs that push you to behave in an uncontrolled manner.

4. Several times a day, especially when you need to exert self-discipline, repeat one of the following affirmations (or create one of your own for the situation) for one or two minutes:

- I am fully in control of myself.
- I have the power to choose my emotions, thoughts, and actions.
- Self-discipline brings me inner strength and leads me to success.
- I am in charge of my behavior.
- I am the master of my life.
- Self-discipline is fun and pleasurable.

5. Use the *V* in your Life S.A.V.E.R.S. to visualize yourself acting with self-discipline. Think of an instance where you usually act with a lack of discipline and visualize yourself acting calmly and with self-mastery.

How is your self-esteem doing?

Self-esteem is having respect for yourself. Healthy or positive self-esteem can help you hold your head high and feel proud of yourself and your actions even when things aren't going well. Self-esteem gives you the courage to try new things and the power to believe in yourself. My success has been directly influenced by my self-esteem, and I know that having it can mean success, and a lack of it can mean failure. If your business isn't growing at the rate you'd like, lack of self-esteem might be the cause. As Maxwell Maltz, the author of *Psycho-Cybernetics*, said, "Low self-esteem is like driving through life with your hand-brake on."

It is vitally important that you give yourself permission to feel proud of yourself. In fact, I'm going to let you in on a secret that some might consider to be a little vain. When I do something that I'm proud of, I often review it multiple times. Let's say I crafted an email to my team or to a prospect that I thought was really good. I'll reread that email several times and possibly save it for future review. If I give a presentation or record a video that I thought came out really well, I'll watch it not only to critique it, but also to bask a little in the parts that I'm proud of. To me, it's similar to doing affirmations. I'm reminding myself of what I like about me, and that's really what self-esteem is all about. Yes, we need to be realistic about our weaknesses and always strive to improve, but don't hesitate to be proud of your strengths and revel in the wins a little.

As you read this book, and I suggest you read it more than once, I recommend that you systematically address areas where you know you need improvement and expansion. If your self-esteem levels could use some boosting, then take steps to elevate them. Design affirmations to increase and develop them over time. Visualize yourself acting with more confidence, raising your personal standards, and loving yourself more. Your self-esteem will rise to match your vision.

An unstoppable self-esteem is a powerful tool. You probably already know that with a negative attitude you are going nowhere—and fast! There's no question that entrepreneurs encounter more avoidance and rejection than the average person. In fact, if you're working on growing your business correctly, you're facing rejection all the time!

Without the right attitude, all that rejection can take its toll. You'll face constant no's and some people won't answer your calls. To face that every day requires a bulletproof level of self-esteem.

Principle #2: Prioritize Fitness and Make Exercise Enjoyable

On a scale of one to 10, where would you rank your health and fitness? Are you fit? Strong? Do you *feel* good more often than not?

How about your energy level throughout the day? Do you have more energy than you know what to do with? Can you wake up before your alarm and do what's important, handle all the demands of the day, and put out the inevitable fires, all without struggling to make it through the day feeling exhausted and out of breath?

I covered exercise as the *E* in S.A.V.E.R.S., and yes, I'm going to discuss it again right now. It's a fact that the state of your health and fitness is a huge factor in your energy and success levels—

especially for entrepreneurs. Because, unlike employees, you're not paid based on the times you clock in and out. You're paid based on the quality of the results you produce within the time you work. Being an entrepreneur is truly an energy sport. Like any sport, you need an extraordinary supply of energy and stamina.

It's no surprise, then, that three priorities of top performers are the quality of what they eat, their sleep, and their exercise, and you need to master each of these. I'll delve deeper into each in the next chapter on Energy Engineering, but let's start with making sure you get your daily exercise in, and the key to that is to find physical activities you actually enjoy doing.

Make exercise enjoyable. The correlation between physical fitness, happiness, and success are undeniable. It is no coincidence that you rarely see top performers who are terribly out of shape. Most schedule and invest 30–60 minutes of their time each day to hit the gym or the running trail because they understand the important role that daily exercise plays in their success.

While the *E* in S.A.V.E.R.S. ensures that you're going to start each day with 5–10 minutes of exercise, I recommended that you make a commitment to engage in additional 30–60 minute workouts at least three to five times per week. Doing so will make certain that your fitness level supports the energy and confidence you need to succeed.

Even better, is to engage in some form of exercise that brings you a deep level of enjoyment. Whether that means going for a hike in nature, playing ultimate frisbee, or getting an exercise bike and putting it in front of your TV so you can enjoy your favorite episode of *Breaking Bad* and forget that you're exercising. Or, do what Hal does: he loves wakeboarding and playing basketball—two excellent forms of exercise—so he does one of them every workday. You'll actually get to see Hal's foundational schedule in the coming pages, so you'll know how those activities fit with the rest of his priorities.

What physical activities do you enjoy that you can commit to schedule as part of your daily exercise ritual?

Principle #3: Aim for Financial Freedom

How is your journey toward financial freedom looking? Is your business highly profitable? Are you earning significantly more money each month than you need to survive? Are you able to consistently save, invest, and contribute a significant portion of your income? Are you debt-free with a large reserve that allows you to capitalize on opportunities that come your way and weather any unexpected financial storms? Are you on pace for financial freedom so that your ongoing passive income will exceed your ongoing monthly expenses? If so, congratulations. You are among a very small percentage of entrepreneurs who are genuinely thriving with their finances.

If not, you're not alone. The majority of people have less than $10,000 to their name and an average of $16,000 in unsecured debt. No judgment here if your finances are not yet where you want them to be. I'm simply going to point you right back to Not-So-Obvious Entrepreneurship Principle #1 and encourage you to take 100 percent responsibility for your financial situation.

I've seen and heard every reason for someone to dive deep into debt, fail to save, and not have a nest egg. None of those matter now. Yes, the best time to have started saving a percentage of your income was five, ten, or even twenty years ago. But the next best time is right now. Whether you're 20, 40, 60, or 80 years old, it's never too late to take control of your personal finances. You'll find an incredible boost in energy from taking charge, and you'll be able to use your accumulated savings to create even more wealth because you'll actually have money to invest in new opportunities. Sounds good, right?

There's a good chance that the decision to become an entrepreneur was partially driven by a desire for financial freedom, but it is going to take more than that. I've seen *many* entrepreneurs make millions of dollars and then wind up dead broke because of poor financial decisions. It turns out that learning how to make money is only half the battle. Learning how to *keep* it by saving and investing wisely is the second part of the puzzle, and learning how to create multiple streams of income—so you're never again dependent on only one—is the next level, which we'll cover in the coming pages.

Financial freedom isn't something you achieve overnight. It is a result of developing the mindset and the habits *now* that will take you down the path that leads to financial freedom.

Here are four practical steps you can start taking today to get you started on your path:

1. Set aside 10 percent of your income to save and invest.

This is a must. In fact, I recommend that you start by taking 10 percent of whatever funds you have in the bank right now and putting it into a separate savings account. (Go ahead. I'll wait.) Make whatever adjustments you need to make to your lifestyle to live off 90 percent of your current income. A little discipline and sacrifice goes a long way. As you see that 10 percent add up over time, it gets exciting, and you'll start to *feel* what's possible for the future.

2. Take another 10 percent and give it away.

Most wealthy people give a percentage of their income to causes they believe in. Warren Buffet recently donated $2.8 billion to charity. "There's no shame in making money. There is only shame in not using it to help others," says Jeff Hoffman, the serial entrepreneur who was largely responsible for founding Priceline.com and making it the fastest company to reach $10 billion in sales.

But you don't have to wait until you are wealthy to start this practice. As Tony Robbins said, "If you won't give $1 out of $10, you'll never give $1 million out of $10 million." Can't do 10 percent or the rent check will bounce? Start with 5, 2, or 1 percent. It's not the amount that matters, but developing the mindset and creating the habit that will change your financial future and serve you for the rest of your life. You've got to start teaching your subconscious mind that it can produce an abundant income, that there's more than enough, and that more is always on the way.

3. Continuously develop your money mindset.

As an entrepreneur, money is one of the most important topics for you to master. You can start by adding the following books, which cover various aspects of achieving financial freedom, to your reading list:

- *Profit First: A Simple System to Transform Any Business from a Cash-Eating Monster to a Money-Making Machine* by Mike Michalowicz

- *Secrets of the Millionaire Mind: Mastering the Inner Game of Wealth* by T. Harv Ecker

- *The Total Money Makeover: A Proven Plan for Financial Fitness* by Dave Ramsey

- *The Millionaire Fastlane: Crack the Code to Wealth and Live Rich for a Lifetime* by MJ DeMarco

- *MONEY: Master the Game: 7 Simple Steps to Financial Freedom* by Tony Robbins

- *Think and Grow Rich* by Napoleon Hill

- *Rich Dad Poor Dad* by Robert Kiyosaki

4. Diversify Your Sources of Income.

Whether you are a serial entrepreneur, CEO, independent contractor, or you're still working a 9-to-5 job and dreaming of more, you value financial security in the present and desire financial freedom in the as-soon-as-possible future. Creating one or more additional streams of income is no longer a luxury. In today's unpredictable economy, it has become a necessity.

Diversifying your sources of income, also known as creating multiple streams of income, is one of the best decisions you can make. It is not only crucial to protect yourself from the unavoidable ups and downs of economic cycles, but also to establish a lifetime of financial independence. Due to the financial risks that come from relying on *one* source of income, such as a job or even a business, I highly recommend beginning to focus on creating at least one or more additional sources to generate cash flow.

At 25, Hal began planning his exit strategy to leave a lucrative, hall of fame sales career to pursue his dream of becoming a full-time entrepreneur. While retaining his sales position and the income it generated, he started his first business and his first additional stream of income. He provided sales coaching for both individual sales reps and sales teams. When the economy crashed in 2008, Hal's income was almost entirely dependent on his coaching business. When more than half of his clients couldn't afford to pay for his coaching, and he lost over half of his income, he swore he'd never be dependent on one source of income again.

Year by year, using the step-by-step formula outlined below, Hal has since added nine additional, significant streams of income. These include private and group coaching programs, writing books, keynote speaking, facilitating paid masterminds, podcasting, foreign publishing, franchising and publishing books in *The Miracle Morning* book series, affiliate income, and hosting live events.

Your additional income streams can be active, passive, or a combination of the two. Some may pay you for doing work that you love (active), while others can provide income for you without you having to do much of anything at all (passive). You can diversify your income streams among different industries to protect you against major losses during downturns in one market and allow you to benefit financially from the upswings in another.

Although Hal's approach to creating multiple streams of income mentioned above and outlined below is just one of countless that you could take (e.g., you could buy real estate, leverage the stock market, open brick-and-mortar stores, etc.), the following steps (4.1-4.8) give you a practical, straight forward process to help you begin brainstorming and implementing immediately.

What's important is that you make diversifying your sources of income a priority. Schedule time blocks in your schedule—one hour a day, one day a week, or a few hours every Saturday—so that you can establish additional income sources that bring you monthly income, which will provide financial security in the present, and ultimately financial freedom in the future. Here are the eight steps that Hal has repeatedly implemented, which you can apply, or modify to fit your situation:

4.1 Establish financial security.

Now, this step isn't sexy, but it's imperative. You might think of it as a disclaimer. Don't focus your time and energy on building a *second* source of income until your *primary* source is secure. Whether you have a day job or own your own business, focus on establishing and securing your primary monthly income that will support your expenses before you pursue other steps. In other words, don't "burn the ships," like Cortés, until you've at least established a row boat that will keep you afloat while you're building your yacht.

4.2 Clarify your unique value.

Every person on this planet has unique gifts, abilities, experiences, and value to offer in a way that adds value for others and that they can be highly compensated for. Figure out the knowledge, experience, ability, or solution you have or can create, which others will find value in, and gladly pay you for. Remember, what might be common knowledge for you isn't necessarily for other people. Here are a few ways that you can differentiate your value in the marketplace.

First ... *who you are* and your unique personality will always differentiate your value from that of every other person on Earth. Many people will resonate with your offering better than they will with someone else's offering that's similar or even the same because of your personality.

Second ... *knowledge* is the one thing you can increase relatively quickly. As Tony Robbins wrote in *Money: Master the Game*, "One reason people succeed is that they have knowledge other people don't have. You pay your lawyer or your doctor for the knowledge and skills you lack."

Increasing your knowledge in a specific area is an effective way to increase the value that others will pay you for—either to teach them what you know, or to apply your knowledge on their behalf.

Third ... *packaging* is how you can differentiate your value. When Hal wrote *The Miracle Morning*, he admittedly had to overcome his insecurity around the fact that waking up early wasn't exactly something he invented. He wondered if there would be a market for the book. But as hundreds of thousands of readers have shared, what made the book so impactful is the way that the information was packaged. It was simple and gave people a step-by-step process that made it possible for anyone to significantly improve any area of their life, by simply altering how they start their day. How can you package your offering to appeal to appeal to the people you want to attract?

4.3 Identify your target audience.

Who are you best qualified to serve? With his background as a record-breaking, hall of fame sales rep, Hal determined that he was best qualified to serve fellow sales reps, so he launched his first coaching program. Now he serves a much larger, worldwide audience through *The Miracle Morning* book series and *Best Year Ever Blueprint* live events, and he coaches both first-time and established authors who want to create seven-figure income streams through their book and back end.

Based on the value you can add for others or the problems you can help people solve, who will pay you for the value you can add for them, the solution you can provide, or the results you can help them generate?

4.4 Build a self-sustaining community.

A turning point in Hal's financial life came when he heard self-made multimillionaire Dan Kennedy explain why one of the most valuable assets you'll ever have, as an entrepreneur, is your email list. So always focus on growing and nurturing it. At that time, Hal's email list was non-existent beyond his family and friends. However, he made it a priority.

Ten years later, in addition to taking Dan's advice and growing his email list to well over 100,000 loyal subscribers, he took it a step further by launching and growing one of the most engaged online communities in the world. *The Miracle Morning Community* Facebook has become a case study, currently with over 55,000 members from 70+ countries, and growing exponentially every day. It's not realistic for Hal to be able to facilitate engagement with that many people on his own, nor does he rely on his team to do it. Instead, through trial and error, he figured out how to automate both the growth of the community—to the tune of attracting more than 3,000 new members every month—and he also automated the member interaction, so that the community is able to self-sustain.

Here are a few tips from Hal on creating a self-sustaining community:

First … *choose your platform*. While it's important to focus on building your email list and communicating with your community individually, it's important that you establish a platform through which you can not only consistently add value, but where members of your community can communicate with, and add value for, each other. While this can be facilitated through a membership platform such as Kajabi (Kajabi.com) CMNTY (cmnty.com) Hal has found that using a Facebook group is advantageous for a few key reasons:

- Most people are already logging into Facebook every day.
- The built in functionality of Facebook Groups allows self-managing.
- Other people are on Facebook to stumble across your community.
- Your members can easily share your content, as well as each other's.

Second … *invite people to your community*. You may have noticed in the opening pages of this book, *A Special Invitation from Hal,* which has been a staple in each of the Miracle Morning books. This is the primary method he leverages to consistently invite people to join the Facebook Group. Yours might be a "P.S." in your emails, or a clickable button on your website. In fact, if you go to MiracleMorning.com you'll also see a button there that says JOIN THE COMMUNITY and links back to the Facebook group. Whatever method you choose, make sure it's visible to your clients, prospects, and anyone else you'd like to have in your community.

Third … *prompt your community to engage*. Start by giving all new members simple instructions that compel them to interact with, and add value for, other members. In the *Best Month Ever Challenge* Facebook group, four simple instructions are given: 1) Create a new post that shares your one area/goal/objective that you're committed to improving this month. 2) Leave a positive/ encouraging/helpful comment on someone else's post 3) Watch the BMEC Videos [with links to the videos] 4) Post in the Group Daily [with specific instructions on what to post].

However, Hal recommends keeping it as simple as possible, such as using a POST and COMMENT model. Simply ask new members to *post* one thing that is relevant to them and the community and comment on someone else's post. This format creates a consistent flow of new posts, and engagement within each member's post.

Another highly engaged online community is Jayson Gaignard's *Mastermind Talks Alumni* Facebook group, which is exclusively for attendees of his Mastermind Talks Event (which happens to be where Hal and I met). Jayson guides member engagement with a simple ASK and GIVE model. You're either asking for something (advice, feedback, an introduction, etc.) or giving something (expertise, re-sources, conference tickets, etc.). This format has created a highly engaged, self-sustaining community where members provide ongoing support for one another.

Fourth ... *consistently add value.* Just because your community and its' engagement are self-sustaining, doesn't mean you should dis-engage. In fact, the more you engage, the better. This could be as simple as sharing valuable resources, or your own content, with your community. Hal posts his weekly podcast episode in the group, ev-ery Wednesday, and shares any valuable resources he comes across. You can also delegate your engagement as appropriate. Since Hal can't possible "like" and "comment" on every person's post, he has his team engage as well. He has also appointed "Community Ambassadors" in various countries, to engage with members in each of those countries.

4.5 Ask your community about their challenges and desires.

You can guess and assume what people want and need, invest valuable time in creating it, and then hope that your guess was correct. But remember, hope is rarely the best strategy.

Instead, send email to members of your community or put up a post in your group with a link to a survey (using a free service like SurveyMonkey or Google Forms). Ask the members what they want or need help within the area of value that you've identified. Ask open-ended questions to get the widest range of possibilities or offer multiple- choice questions if you've already thought about what you can provide.

For the most comprehensive guide written on how to use surveys to assess what your audience want and how you can best serve them, I highly recommend Ryan Levesque's book, *Ask: The Counterintuitive Online Formula to Discover Exactly What Your Customers Want to Buy... Create a Mass of Raving Fans... and Take Any Business to the Next Level.*

4.6 Create a solution.

After your community members tell you what they need, it's your golden opportunity to get to work and create it. This could be a physical or digital product (a book, an audio, a video, a written training program, or software) or a service (dog grooming, babysitting, coaching, consulting, speaking, or training).

4.7 Plan the launch.

Think about how Apple rolls out its products. The company doesn't just throw a product on the shelf or up on its website. No, the company makes it into an event. Apple builds anticipation months in advance, so much so that people are willing to camp in front of stores for weeks to be the first in line. To learn how to do this, read the definitive book on the topic, *Launch* by Jeff Walker.

4.8 Find a mentor.

Depending on your level of experience, you may want to make this your *first* step. As you're aware, one of the most effective methods of minimizing your learning curve and maximizing the speed at which you attain a desired result is to find someone who has already achieved that result, and then model their strategy. Rather than try to figure it out on your own, find someone who has already achieved what you want, determine how this person did it, model this behavior, and modify it to fit your needs.

While you may seek a face-to-face or virtual relationship with a mentor, you could also join as mastermind and hire a coach. Even reading a book, like this one, is tapping into the wisdom of a mentor.

Final thoughts … Whether you follow these steps, create a new business, or start buying investment properties, schedule time to begin adding and developing another source of income, and within months you can be enjoying the benefits, the perks and the financial security, peace of mind, and freedom that comes from having multiple streams of income. Two years from now, you'll wish you would have started today. Don't wish and don't wait. Start.

Principle #4: Systematize Your World

In chapters 7–10, I'm going to go in depth on the strategies and systems that I believe will be the most helpful to you as an entrepreneur. However, I don't want to make any assumptions here, so I want to start with some basics. Effective self-leaders have systems for just about everything. From business activities (such as scheduling, follow-up, entering orders, and even showing appreciation for clients and team members) to personal activities (such as sleeping, eating, managing finances, travel, and family responsibilities). Systems make your life easier, ensure you're always ready to perform, and make your tasks more easily delegated to an assistant or other team member.

Here are a few practices you can implement immediately to begin systematizing your world:

1. Foundational Scheduling

There is no doubt that one of the most attractive aspects of entrepreneurship is the opportunity for *freedom*. It's one of the main reasons anyone becomes an entrepreneur—the freedom to do what you want, when you want, and the freedom to earn an extraordinary income as a result. One consequence of the freedom and options for work available these days is that not all entrepreneurs necessarily know how to manage it all. As a result, their focus, productivity, and income suffer from the lifestyle they desire. They spend too many days bouncing from one task to another and end far too many days wondering where the time went and what, if any, significant progress they made. Can you relate?

I am going to share something with you that will transform your ability to produce consistent and spectacular entrepreneurial results. *You must create a foundational schedule that adds structure and intentionality to your days and weeks.* A foundational schedule is a pre-determined, recurring schedule that is made up of focused time blocks dedicated to your highest priority activities.

I know, I know—you became an entrepreneur to get away from structure. Trust me, I understand. But the more you leverage a foundational schedule, consisting of time blocks dedicated to the projects or activities that will move the needle in your business life, the more freedom you'll ultimately create.

That's not to say you cannot have flexibility in your schedule. In fact, I strongly suggest that you *schedule* flexibility. Plan plenty of time blocks for family, fun, and recreation in your calendar. You could even go as far as to include a "whatever I feel like" time block, during which you do, well ... whatever you feel like. You can also move things on occasion as needed.

What's important is that you go through your days and weeks with a high level of clarity and intention about how you're going to invest every hour of every day, even if that hour is spent doing *whatever you feel like*. At least you planned on it. Maintaining a foundational schedule is how you will maximize your productivity so that you almost never end the day wondering where your time went. It won't go anywhere without your making a conscious decision because you'll be intentional with every minute of it.

I asked Hal to share his weekly foundational schedule so you can see an example of what this can look like. Although Hal has the luxury of entrepreneurial freedom and doesn't need to follow any pre-determined schedule, he will tell you that having this foundational schedule in place is one of his keys to ensuring he maximizes each day. If your life has external structure, for example a job with regular hours while you build your business, you can structure your time off and probably some of your work time as well. One thing you'll notice about this schedule is that every hour is planned, whether it is time off or time for work.

HAL'S FOUNDATIONAL SCHEDULE

Time	Mon	Tues
4:00 AM	SAVERS	SAVERS
5:00 AM	Write	Write
6:00 AM	Emails	Emails
7:00 AM	Take kids to school	Take kids to school
8:00 AM	Staff Mtg.	#1 Priority
9:00 AM	#1 Priority	Wakeboard
↓	↓	↓
11:00 AM	Lunch	Lunch
12:00 PM	Basketball	Priorities
1:00 PM	Priorities	Interview
2:00 PM	Priorities	Interview
3:00 PM	Priorities	Interview
4:00 PM	Priorities	Priorities
5:00 PM	FAMILY	FAMILY
↓	↓	↓
10:00 PM	Bed	Bed

(Note: Every hour is planned.)

Wed	Thurs	Fri	Sat/Sun
SAVERS	SAVERS	SAVERS	SAVERS
Write	Write	Write	Write
Emails	Emails	Emails	↓
Take kids to school	Take kids to school	Take kids to school	FAMILY Time
#1 Priority	#1 Priority	#1 Priority	↓
↓	Wakeboard	↓	↓
↓	↓	↓	↓
Lunch	Lunch	Lunch	↓
Basketball	Priorities	Basketball	↓
Client Call	Interview	Priorities	↓
Client Call	Interview	Priorities	↓
Client Call	Interview	Priorities	↓
Priorities	Priorities	PLANNING	↓
FAMILY	FAMILY	Date Night	↓
↓	↓	↓	↓
Bed	Bed	:^) ???	Bed

Keep in mind that, like most entrepreneurs, things come up that cause Hal's foundational schedule to change (events, speaking engagements, vacations, etc.), but only temporarily. As soon as he's back home and in his office, this is the schedule he falls back into.

One of the main reasons this technique is so effective is it takes the emotional roller coaster out of the decision making for your daily activities. How many times has an appointment or meeting gone badly and then affected your emotional state and your ability to focus for the rest of the day? Chances are, it happens more often than you'd like to admit. If you followed a foundational schedule you were committed to, and the calendar said networking event, writing ads, or making calls, then you would have a fruitful afternoon. Take control. Stop leaving your productivity to chance and letting outside influences manage your time. Create your foundational schedule—one that incorporates everything you need to get done, as well as recreational, family and fun time—and follow through with it no matter what.

If you find you need additional support to ensure that you follow through, send a copy of your foundational schedule to an accountability partner and have them hold you accountable. Your commitment to this one system will allow you to have significantly more control over your productivity and results.

2. Systematizing Travel

Hal and I are both keynote speakers and regularly spend time on planes and in hotels, around the country and abroad to share what we've learned with others. We have both found that remembering, collecting, and packing all the items we need for every trip is time-consuming, inefficient, and ineffective because it wouldn't be uncommon to forget a necessary item at home or in the office.

We've each assembled a prepacked travel bag that contains every item we need for our trips. From business attire, socks, underwear, and a swimsuit to backup adaptors and chargers for our phones and computers. We even include an assortment of healthy snacks and earplugs (in case one of our hotel room neighbors is excessively noisy). We can leave home at a moment's notice because our bags already contain everything we need to conduct business on the road.

If you're not much of a business traveler, you can still use systems to make your day go more smoothly. You could pack your lunch, gym bag, or purse at night before you go to bed. Or prepare an out-of-office kit with books, brochures, catalogs, or other items you need for business. Where else might you incorporate a system for something you do regularly so you can ensure that you're always prepared without having to invest mental energy each time?

3. Systematizing Accountability

The link between success and accountability is irrefutable. Virtually all highly successful people—from CEOs and professional athletes to the president of the United States—embrace a high degree of accountability. It gives them the leverage they need to take action and create results, even when they don't feel like it. Without leverage, more athletes would skip practice, and CEOs would spend their days playing games on their phones.

Accountability is the act of being responsible to someone else for some action or result. Very little happens in this world, or in your life, without some form of accountability. Virtually every positive result you and I have achieved from birth to age eighteen was thanks to the accountability provided for us by the adults in our lives (parents, teachers, coaches, etc.) We ate our vegetables, completed homework, brushed our teeth, bathed, and got to bed at a reasonable hour. If it weren't for the accountability provided for us by our parents and teachers, we might have been uneducated, malnourished, sleep-deprived, dirty little kids! Nice way to reframe it, right?

Accountability brings order to our lives and allows us to progress, improve, and achieve results we wouldn't have otherwise. Here's the problem: accountability was never something you and I asked for, but something we endured as children, teens, and young adults. Because it was forced upon us by adults, most of us unconsciously grew to resist and resent accountability altogether. Then as we grew into adulthood, we embraced every ounce of freedom we could get, continuing to avoid accountability like the plague, perpetuating a downward spiral into mediocrity, and developing detrimental mindsets and habits—hardly a recipe for success.

Now that we are all grown up and striving to achieve ever higher levels of success and fulfillment, we must take responsibility for initiating our own systems for accountability (or move back in with our parents). Your accountability system could be a professional coach, mentor, a good friend, or family member.

Accountability helps to drive focus. It doesn't let you get away with excuses you might otherwise tell yourself because you've made a commitment to your goals *and* to someone else. The way I create accountability for myself as an entrepreneur is by posting my top three goals each day to another business owner. I use a free app called CommitTo3. Every morning, I exchange my list of top three business goals using this app with my friend Joe Polish, who is the founder of the Genius Network. We let each other know what we want to accomplish by day's end. I do the same thing with another friend of mine, Gordie Bufton, with my personal goals. Knowing I have to account for these three goals by the end of the day—or admit to my friends that I didn't achieve them—keeps me from getting sidetracked along the way.

4. Automating Appreciation

If you've seen me speak or read my blog, you may have heard the story of the "Mind Blowing Door Opener." In case you haven't, prepare to have your mind blown or at least hear how my mind was.

Six years ago I was speaking at the 20th anniversary of the Entrepreneurs Organization (EO) in Las Vegas. It is not unusual for people to come up after I present to say hello, ask questions, or ask for my contact info. It's not a big deal, and it usually doesn't result in much more than a few seconds of interaction. But this time was different.

A young EO guy I'd never met before named John Ruhlin engaged me in conversation. He asked if I was traveling to Cleveland to speak at an EO chapter meeting the following week and, if so, what my plans were for the evening before. I told him I was coming to his city and that I would more than likely take advantage of the opportunity to shop at my favorite store, Brooks Brothers.

We made plans to have dinner and see a Cavs basketball game after my shopping trip. Offering dinner and a sporting event is a nice gesture in business, but not a big deal or out of the ordinary, right?

Well as it turned out, that day was a traveler's nightmare. With multiple delays, I had to beg my way onto a flight that was pulling away from the jetway. I texted John to let him know that I was coming in five hours later than expected and that I understood if he wanted to cancel. He casually reassured me that it was no problem and that he was waiting at the bar in my hotel. He said I should check in, take my bags upstairs, and come down refreshed for a great night. I thought, even though I wouldn't get to go shopping, I could still enjoy a great meal and take in a little LeBron James. All in all, not a bad way to spend an evening in Cleveland. That is what I was expecting ...

I arrived at the hotel, and when I went to walk into my room, my jaw dropped. Spread out folded and hanging across my entire room were dozens of suit jackets, pants, shirts, and sweaters. Not just any dress clothes, they were *Brooks Brothers* dress clothes. My entire room looked like I had walked into the retail store. And it was all in my size.

Then it hit me like a ton of bricks. John, the EO guy, had casually asked me what size I wore in an email that week because he said he wanted to send me his company T-shirt.

He'd just pulled off this amazing, mind-altering experience of service—what he calls strategic appreciation—and we weren't even at dinner yet. I took as many pictures on my phone as I could, texted my wife, and realized I needed to call John DiJulius to change the example I had given him for his book about customer service.

When I walked into the bar, John looked up with a grin and said, "You enjoyed your Brooks Brothers store?"

Over dinner and during the game, John explained how using ultra high-end gifts helps him land meetings with CEOs and keep top client relationships amazing. He even wrote the book on it, *Giftology: The Art and Science of Using Gifts to Cut Through the Noise, Increase Referrals, and Strengthen Retention.*

One of John's companies, Ruhlin Group, specializes in automating appreciation and sends customized, personalized, high quality gifts to clients, prospects, and employees on your behalf. Or, if you want to make a connection with a CEO, John's company might send a $500 Cutco knife set in five consecutive packages to the CEO asking them to *carve out time* for a meeting. Hal and I use John and his company to automate all of our gifting.

After the Brooks Brothers experience, and the awesome Ruhlin Group gifts, I will meet Ruhlin anytime, anyplace, and refer him to anybody because I can only hope more and more people get to experience the Ruhlin Group treatment first hand.

5. Clothing Optional

No, this is not about whether to wear clothing but what you wear. I suggest that you consider taking entrepreneurial fashion tips from Steve Jobs and Mark Zuckerberg. Both are famous for wearing the same thing, day in and day out, to keep things simple and give them one less, relatively insignificant decision to make. Zuckerberg typically shows up to work wearing a grey T-shirt or hoodie sweatshirt with a pair of jeans. While Jobs, the late Apple CEO, was known for his signature black turtleneck with jeans. He even tried to go as far as having his whole company wear the same uniform at one point, according to Walter Isaacson's biography.

Tucker Max, CEO of Book In A Box, can be seen sporting the same Lululemon shorts and T-shirt, day in and day out, no matter where he is. I've seen him take the stage to speak at multiple high level entrepreneur events, and his attire never waivers.

Similarly, Hal owns 23 identical black v-neck T-shirts, which he almost always pairs with Lululemon pants.

So, what gives? Obviously these entrepreneurs can afford to own a wide variety of clothing. But they realize that we all have limited brain power, which the latest research has shown is depleted throughout the day, with each decision that we make. (Remember what I mentioned about ego depletion earlier?) The more you can systematize your world and the fewer decisions you have to make, the more brain power you'll have in the tank to make the ones that count.

I've shared five solid ideas to help you systematize your life. But where to from here? You'll know you need a system when you have a recurring challenge or you find that you're missing opportunities because you're unprepared. Said another way, wherever you feel like you're dropping the ball or experiencing habitual stress, you need a system. The more you leverage systems, the less you have to think, and the more you'll be able to get done. We'll cover more in depth ways to systematize your world in the coming chapters, including how to leverage yourself up by getting COO.

Principle #5: Commit to Your Result-Producing Process

If there is any not-so-obvious secret to success in business, this is it: Clarify, calculate, and commit to your result-producing process—*without being emotionally attached to your results.*

Every result that you desire, from improving your physique to growing your business, is preceded by a process, and it's your process that is necessary and responsible for producing your desired results.

When you clarify, calculate, and commit to your result-producing process, and commit to it for an extended period, the results take care of themselves. There's no need to stress or worry about how a day, a week, a month, or even a year goes—so long as you're committed to your process for the long haul. The law of averages always prevails.

Yet, as human beings, it is natural for us to be emotionally attached to our results. As entrepreneurs, we can let a bad day on the phone, an underperforming product launch, a client canceling our services, or any other less than optimal result discourage us. We allow bad results cause us to feel bad. When our numbers are down, we feel down. We ride the emotional roller coaster of being an entrepreneur, and our emotional attachment to our results negatively affects our commitment to the process. But does it have to be that way? It absolutely does not.

Hal had the following realization, at just 21 years old, to which he credits much of the success he achieved during his record breaking, hall of fame sales career. This is also the core principle that enabled him to lead his sales team to break Cutco's annual sales record, becoming the first team in the 55-year history of the company to produce over $2 million in a single year. "My breakthrough occurred when, as a sales rep, I realized that I could predict and control my sales results, by clarifying, calculating, and committing to the process that was responsible for producing those results.

"First, I clarified that my results-producing process was making phone calls to prospects. Simple. Next, I calculated precisely how many calls I needed to make to prospects, based on my averages, to reach my sales goals. Then I realized that all I had to do was make an unwavering commitment to follow through with that predetermined number of calls each day, and then the law of averages would all but assure I would reach my sales goals each month, quarter, and year. Finally, I made a conscious decision to let go of any emotional attachment to my day-to-day results because I was focused on the bigger picture."

A bad day on the phone, or in the field … who cares? A canceled order, disgruntled customer, or even losing a key employee … it doesn't matter in the long run. Why stress over how a day, week, or even a month goes when you're in it for the long haul? Wait, you are in it for the long haul, aren't you? Of course you are!

But be sure to listen to the crucial piece of this strategy: "I realized that any increase I made in my process would cause an almost identical increase in my results. For example, if I doubled the number of calls I made, I would automatically double my sales. It almost seemed too simple, but it worked like clockwork. Focusing on doubling your best results can be scary, but increasing your time for daily calls from one hour to two is easy. I applied this to managing my sales team's daily calls (which they were responsible for tracking and reporting to our management team), and we doubled the entire organization's sales."

Entrepreneurs who consistently predict and produce exceptional results know their numbers and take consistent action —whether they feel like it or not—to leverage those numbers. In the chapters that follow, I'll give you further insight and direction to help you know where to focus your efforts. For now, I encourage you to take time to *clarify, calculate, and commit to your result-producing process* and make the conscious decision to do so *without being emotionally attached to your results.*

Putting Self-Leadership into Action

1. **Take 100 Percent Responsibility.** Remember, the moment you accept responsibility for *everything* in your life is the moment you claim the power to change *anything* in your life. Your success is 100 percent up to you.

2. **Prioritize Health and Fitness First.** If daily fitness isn't already a priority in your life, make it so. In addition to your morning exercise, make time for longer 30- to 60-minute workouts three to five times each week. As for which foods will give you a surplus of energy, we'll cover that in the next chapter.

3. **Aim for Financial Freedom.** Begin to develop the mindset and habits that will inevitably lead you to a life of financial freedom, including saving a minimum of 10 percent of your income, continuously educating yourself on the topic of money, and diversifying your sources of income.

4. **Systematize Your World.** Start by creating a foundational schedule and then identify what areas of your life or business can benefit from systems and time-blocked schedules so that every day your result-producing processes have been predetermined, and your success is virtually guaranteed. Make sure you add a system for accountability in your world whether that is through a colleague, a coach, or by leveraging your team.

5. **Commit to Your Results-Producing Process.** Remember Hal's not-so-obvious secret to success: *clarify, calculate, and commit to your process without being emotionally attached to your results.* Make your success inevitable by staying committed to your process each day, and let go of any emotional attachment to your short-term results since it's your

commitment to your (and your team's) daily process that will determine your revenue at the end of the month, quarter, and year.

By now I hope you've gained a sense of how critical these five core principles are to your success as an entrepreneur. Remember, taking your business to the next level starts with taking yourself to the next level. It only happens in that order.

Next, we're going to focus on how to engineer your life to create optimal levels of sustained physical, mental, and emotional energy so that you're able to maintain extraordinary levels of clarity, focus, and action day in and day out.

Entrepreneur Profile

Ari Meisel

Ari Meisel's company is Less Doing.

Top Business Accomplishments

❖ Ari is a two-time best-selling author.

❖ He launched a company in 48 hours that was scalable and profitable from day one and that grew at 20 percent per month.

❖ Ari created a brand new system of productivity called Less Doing.

❖ He has been called a world-class productivity expert by Tony Robbins, Joe Polish, Daymond John, and Jordan Belfort.

❖ He created a business that supports his life with his wife and four kids, instead of the other way around.

Morning Routine

❖ Ari wakes at 5:15 a.m.

❖ He checks Slack, Trello, Gmail, and Facebook. Plenty of people recommend avoiding these tasks first thing in the morning, but Ari finds it takes him five to eight minutes, and he can get a ton of balls in motion, which energizes him for the day. (He doesn't look at his phone again until his kids are off to school.)

❖ He makes a morning smoothie, and then he makes breakfast for his kids and takes them to school.

❖ To sum up, he does 10 minutes of high-impact, high-efficiency work, has three and a half hours of family time, and *then* he starts his workday.

— 5 —

ENTREPRENEUR ELEVATION SKILL #2:
ENERGY ENGINEERING

The world belongs to the energetic.
—RALPH WALDO EMERSON

A s an entrepreneur, you live and die by your own steam. You eat what you kill as they say. The trouble, though, isn't that it's all up to you. On some days—and I know you've had those days—you wake up, and you just don't have the energy or the motivation to hunt. To maintain your focus on those days, in the midst of uncertainty and overwhelm, is no easy task. The good days take energy, enthusiasm, and persistence. The hard days? Take all that and more.

An entrepreneur with low energy suffers greatly. Motivation is hard to sustain. Focus is often generated artificially by stimulants, such as the entrepreneur's drug of choice, caffeine. *Entrepreneurship requires an abundance of energy.* There's no way around it. You can have the best product, the most amazing team, and the most effective marketing, but if you don't have the *energy* to engage and manage it all, you're going to crash. If you want to maximize your success in business, you need energy—the more the better, and the more *consistent* the better.

- Energy is the fuel that enables you to maintain clarity, focus, and action so that you can generate results day after day.

- Energy is contagious. It spreads from you to your clients and prospects like a positive virus, creating symptoms of enthusiasm and affirmative responses everywhere.

- Energy is a vaccine against rejection and disappointment. Have enough of it, and you're almost permanently inoculated against negativity.

The question then becomes, *how do you strategically engineer your life so that you maintain a high level of sustainable energy, which is always available to you, on demand?*

When I'm struggling with energy issues, I can compensate with caffeine and other stimulants, and they'll work for a while … until I crash. You may have noticed the same thing. The energy seems to fall off just when you need it the most. Can't you just hear one of those infomercial hosts chime in here: *But Cameron, there's got to be a better way!*

There is …

If you have been, until now, fueling yourself on coffee and pure determination, you haven't even begun to reach the heights of achievement that are possible when you begin to engineer your life for optimum energy.

Natural Energy Cycles

The first thing to understand about energy is that the goal isn't to be running at full speed all the time. It isn't practical to maintain a constant output. As human beings, we have a natural ebb and flow to our energy levels. Entrepreneurship, it turns out, is the same. The trick is to marry, or at least try to sync up, your cycles with the rhythm of your work day. Know that you will need to access deeper wells of energy during particularly intense times throughout the week, month, and year and allow yourself the time to rest, rejuvenate, and recharge when the intensity lessens.

Just like houseplants need water, our energy reserves need regular replenishing. You can go full tilt for long periods of time, but eventually your mind, body, and spirit will need to be refilled. Think of your life as a container that holds your energy. When you do not properly manage what's in your container, it's like having a hole in the bottom. No matter how much you pour in, you still won't feel fully energized.

If you have resigned yourself to being tired, cranky, behind on your to-do list, out of shape, and unhappy, I have some great news.

Being continually exhausted is not only unacceptable, *you don't have to settle for it.* There are a few simple ways to get what you need and want—more rest, time to replenish and recharge, and inner peace and happiness. A tall order? Yes. Impossible? Heck, no!

This is about strategically engineering your life for optimum and sustainable physical, mental, and emotional energy. Here are the three principles I follow to keep my energy reserves at maximum capacity and on tap for whenever I need them.

1. Eat and Drink for Energy

When it comes to energy engineering, what you eat and drink may play the most critical role of all. If you're like most people, you base your food choices on taste first and the consequences second (if you consider them at all). Yet, what pleases our taste buds in the moment doesn't always give us maximum energy to last throughout the day.

There is nothing wrong with eating foods that taste good, but if you want to be truly healthy and have the energy to perform like a champion, here's the big idea: it is crucial that we make a conscious decision to **place more value on the health and energy**

consequences of food than we do on the taste. Why? Because digesting food is one of the most energy-draining processes that the body endures. Need evidence? Think about how exhausted you feel after a big meal, like Thanksgiving dinner. It's no coincidence that a large meal is usually followed by heavy eyes and ultimately a nap. They call it a food coma for a reason.

Digesting foods like bread, cooked meats, dairy products, and any foods that have been processed, requires more energy than they contribute to your body. So, rather than giving you energy, these essentially "dead" foods tend to drain your energy to fuel digestion and leave you with an energy deficit. On the other hand, "living" foods, like raw fruits, vegetables, nuts, and seeds typically give you more energy than they require for digestion, and therefore provide your body and mind with an energy surplus, which enables you to perform at your best.

Put very simply, everything you put in your body either contributes to or detracts from your health and energy. Drinking water puts a check in the plus column; double shots of tequila won't. Eating a diet rich with fresh fruits and vegetables equals more plusses. Rolling through the drive-through to wolf down some fast food? Not so much. I know you know the drill. This isn't rocket science, but it may be the single most important area of your life to optimize. You may need to stop fooling yourself.

If you're not already doing so, it's time to be intentional and strategic about what you eat, when you eat, and most importantly —*why* you eat—so that you can engineer your life for optimum energy.

Strategic Eating

Up until this point, you may have been wondering, *when do I get to eat during my Miracle Morning?!* I'll cover that here. I'll also share *what* to eat for maximum energy, which is critical, and *why* you choose to eat what you eat may be most important consideration of all.

When To Eat—Again, remember that digesting food uses a lot of energy each day. The bigger the meal, the more food you give your body to digest, the more drained you will feel. With that in mind, I recommend eating your first meal *after* your Miracle Morning. This ensures that, for optimum alertness and focus during the Life S.A.V.E.R.S., your blood will be flowing to your brain rather than to your stomach to digest your food.

However, I do recommend starting your day by ingesting a small amount of healthy fats as fuel for your brain. Studies show that keeping your mind sharp and your moods in balance may be largely related to the type of fat you eat. "Our brain is at least 60 percent fat, and it's composed of fats (like omega-3s) that must be obtained from the diet," says Amy Jamieson-Petonic, MEd, a registered dietitian, the director of wellness coaching at the Cleveland Clinic, and a national spokesperson for the American Dietetic Association.

After drinking his first full glass of water, Hal starts every morning with a tablespoon of organic coconut butter (specifically *Nutiva Organic Coconut Manna*, which you can order from Amazon.com) and a large mug of organic coffee, which he blends with Bulletproof Cacao Butter (available on Bulletproof.com). The tablespoon of coconut butter is such a small amount that it's easily digested, and it contains enough healthy fats to provide fuel for the brain. The health benefits of cacao are significant, from lowering blood pressure to being a powerhouse full of antioxidants (cacao rates in the top 20 on the oxygen radical absorbance capacity "ORAC" scale, which is used to rate the antioxidant capacity of foods).

Maybe most exciting fact is that, eating cacao actually makes you happy! It contains phenylethylamine (known as the "love drug"), which is responsible for the state of our mood and the same feelings you get when you are in love. It also acts as a stimulant and can improve mental alertness. In other words, cacao equals win, win, win!

If you feel that you must eat a meal first thing in the morning, make sure that it's a small, light, and easily digestible meal, such as fresh fruit or a smoothie (more on that in a minute).

Why To Eat—Let's take a moment to delve deeper into *why* you choose to eat the foods that you do. When you're shopping at the grocery store or selecting food from a menu at a restaurant, what criteria do you use to determine which foods you are going to put in your body? Are your choices based purely on taste? Texture? Convenience? Are they based on health? Energy? Dietary restrictions?

Most people choose the foods they eat based solely on the *taste*, and at a deeper level, because of an emotional attachment to the foods they like the taste of. If you were to ask someone why they eat ice cream or fried chicken or drink soda, they would most likely say that they love ice cream, were in the mood for fried chicken, or like drinking soda. All of these answers are based on the emotional enjoyment derived primarily from the way these foods taste. In this case, a person is not likely to explain their food choices with how much value these foods will add to their health, or how much sustained energy they'll receive as a result of ingesting them.

My point is this: if we want to have more energy (which we all do), and if we want our lives to be healthy and disease-free (which we all do), then it is crucial that we reexamine why we eat the foods that we do. From this point forward—and I know I've covered this, but it bears repeating—*start placing significantly more value on the health and energy consequences of the foods you eat than you do on the taste*. The taste provides you with only a few minutes of pleasure, but the health and energy consequences impact the rest of your day and the rest of your life.

In no way am I saying that we should eat foods that don't taste good in exchange for the health and energy benefits. I'm saying that we can have both. If we want to live every day with an abundance of energy so we can perform at our best and live long, healthy lives, we must choose to eat more foods that are good for our health and give us sustained energy as well as taste great.

What To Eat—Before we talk about what to eat, let's take a second to talk about what to *drink*. Remember that Step #4 of the *Five-Step, Snooze-Proof, Wake-Up Strategy* is to drink a full glass of water first thing in the morning so you can rehydrate and re-energize after a full night of sleep.

Next, like Hal, I typically brew a cup of Bulletproof Coffee before I start my Miracle Morning. I set my alarm 15 minutes early to give myself time to make my coffee without intruding on my time for the S.A.V.E.R.S.

As for what to eat, it has been proven that a diet rich in *living foods*, such as fresh fruits and vegetables will greatly increase your energy levels, improve your mental focus and emotional well being, keep you healthy, and protect you from disease. Hal created the Miracle Morning "Super-Food Smoothie" that incorporates everything your body needs in one tall, frosty glass! I'm talking about complete protein (*all* the essential amino acids), age defying antioxidants, Omega 3 essential fatty acids (to boost immunity, cardiovascular health, and brain power), plus a rich spectrum of vitamins and minerals … and that's just for starters. I haven't even mentioned all the *super-foods*, such as the stimulating, mood-lifting phytonutrients in Cacao (the tropical bean from which chocolate is made), the long-lasting energy of Maca (the Andean adaptogen revered for its hormone-balancing effects), and the immune-boosting nutrients and appetite-suppressing properties of Chia seeds.

The Miracle Morning Super-Food Smoothie not only provides you with sustained energy, it also tastes great. You might even find that it enhances your ability to create miracles in your everyday life. You can download and print the recipe for free at www.TMMBook.com.

Remember the old saying "you are what you eat"? Food provides the building blocks and the fuel your body needs to do all the amazing things it does. Take care of your body so your body will take care of you. You will feel vibrant energy and enhanced clarity immediately!

Let's talk about fuel. I have shifted my view of food from that of a reward, treat, or comfort, to that of fuel. I want to eat delicious, healthy foods that boost my energy levels and allow me to keep going as long as I need and want to go.

Don't get me wrong. I still enjoy certain foods that are not the healthiest choices, but I strategically reserve them for times when I don't need to maintain optimal energy levels, such as in the evenings and on weekends.

The easiest way to start making better decisions about eating is to start paying attention to the way you feel after eating certain foods. I started setting a timer for 60 minutes after I finished each meal. When my timer went off, I assessed my energy level. It didn't take long for me to recognize which foods gave me the biggest power boost and which ones didn't. I can clearly tell the difference in my energy level on the days when I drink a smoothie or eat a salad and the day I cave for a chicken sandwich or some of that pizza that smells so good. The former gives me a surplus of energy, the latter put me in an energy deficit.

What would it be like to give your body what it needs to work and play for as long as you like? What would it be like to give yourself exactly what you truly deserve? Give yourself the gift of great health, consciously chosen through what you eat and drink.

If you are eating throughout the day almost as an afterthought, maybe hitting a drive-through after you've hit the point of being famished, it is time to start building a new strategy.

Give some thought to the following:

- Can I start to consciously consider the consequences of what I eat (both health and energy consequences) and value that above the taste?

- Can I keep water with me at all times so that I can hydrate with intention and purpose and avoid becoming dehydrated?

- Can I plan my meals in advance, including incorporating healthy snacks, so I can combat any patterns I have that don't serve me?

Yes, you can do all of these and much more. Think about how much better your life will be and how much more energy you will have for your business when you become conscious and intentional about your eating and drinking habits.

- You will easily maintain a positive mental and emotional state. Low energy causes us to feel down, whereas high energy levels produce a positive state of mind, outlook, and attitude.

- You will be more disciplined. Low energy drains our willpower, making us more likely to choose the *easy* things over the *right* things. High energy levels increase self-discipline.

- You will set an example for the people you lead and the people you love. How we live our lives give permission to those around us to do the same.

- You will get healthier, feel much better, and live longer.

- Bonus—You will settle at your natural weight effortlessly.

- Best Bonus Ever—You'll grow your business faster, make more sales, recruit more and better team members, and make more money because you'll look and feel great!

Don't forget to stay hydrated throughout the day. Lack of water can lead to dehydration, a condition that occurs when you don't have enough water in your body to carry out normal functions. Even mild dehydration can drain your energy and make you tired.

By implementing the Five-Step, Snooze-Proof, Wake-Up Strategy, you'll have had your first glass of water at the start of the day. Beyond that, I recommend keeping a large water bottle with you at all times, and make a habit of drinking 16 ounces every one to two hours. If remembering to drink is a challenge for you, set a recurring timer to trigger the habit to finish your water bottle and refill it for the next round of rehydration.

When it comes to frequency of eating, it's important to refuel every three to four hours, with small, easily digestible, living foods. I intentionally refuel every three to four hours during the day. My regular meals consist of some form of protein and vegetables. To keep my blood glucose levels from dropping, I snack frequently on living foods, including raw fruits and nuts, and one of my favorite go-to snack—kale chips. I try to plan my best meals for the days I need to be the most productive.

I believe that eating for energy—from my first meal of the day, until I'm done working—combined with exercise, also gives me the freedom to eat what I want in the evenings and on weekends. I believe I can eat whatever I want just not always as much as I'd like. I've learned to taste everything but eat just enough that I'm satisfied.

In the end, here is the simple thing to remember: food is fuel. We should use it to get us from the beginning of the day all the way to the end, feeling great and having plenty of energy. Placing more value on the energy consequences of the foods you eat, above the taste, and eating foods that fuel energy, is the first step in energy engineering.

2. Sleep and Wake to Win

Sleep more to achieve more. That might be the most counter-intuitive mantra you'll ever hear, but it's true. The body needs enough shut-eye each night to function properly and to recharge after a demanding day. Sleep also plays a critical role in immune function, metabolism, memory, learning, and other vital bodily functions. It's when the body does the majority of its repairing, healing, resting, and growing.

If you don't sleep enough, you're gradually wearing yourself down and limiting your ability to grow in any part of your life.

Sleeping Versus Sleeping Enough

But how much is enough? There is a big difference between the amount of sleep you can get by on and the amount you need to function optimally. Researchers at the University of California, San Francisco discovered that some people have a gene that enables them to do well on six hours of sleep a night. This gene, however, is very rare, appearing in less than 3 percent of the population. For the other 97 percent of us, six hours doesn't come close to cutting it. Just because you're able to function on five to six hours of sleep doesn't mean you wouldn't feel a lot better and actually get more done if you spent an extra hour or two in bed.

That may sound counterintuitive. You might be thinking *spend more time in bed and get more done? How does that work?* But it has been well documented that enough sleep allows the body to function at higher levels of performance. You'll not only work better and faster, but your attitude will improve, too.

The amount of rest each individual needs every night differs, but research shows that the average adult needs approximately seven to eight hours of sleep to restore the energy it takes to handle all the demands of living each day.

I have been conditioned, as many of us have, to think I need eight to ten hours of sleep. In fact, sometimes I need less, and sometimes I need more. The best way to figure out if you're meeting your sleep needs is to evaluate how you feel as you go about your day. If you're logging enough hours, you'll feel energetic and alert all day long, from the moment you wake up until your regular bedtime. If you're not, you'll reach for caffeine or sugar midmorning or midafternoon ... or both.

If you're like most people, when you don't get enough rest, you have difficulty concentrating, thinking clearly, and even remembering things. You might notice your ineffectiveness or inefficiencies at home or at work or even blame these missteps on your busy schedule. The more sleep you miss, the more pronounced your symptoms become.

In addition, a lack of rest and relaxation can really work a number on your mood. Entrepreneurship is no place for crankiness! It is a scientific fact that when individuals miss out on good nightly rest, their personalities are affected, and they are generally grumpier, less patient, and snap at people more easily. The result of missing out on critical, much-needed rest might make you a bear to be around, which is not much fun for anyone, yourself included.

Most adults cut back on their sleep to pack more activities into their day. As you run against the clock to beat deadlines, you might be tempted to skimp on sleep to get more done. Unfortunately, lack of sleep can cause the body to run down, which allows illness, viruses, and diseases the tiny opening they need to attack the body. When you are sleep deprived, your immune system can become compromised, and is susceptible to just about anything. Eventually, lack of rest can cause illness that leads to missed days or even weeks of work. That's no way to attempt to grow your business.

On the flip side, when you get enough sleep, your body runs as it should, you're pleasant to be around, and your immune system is stronger. And that's precisely when you'll make more sales and attract more people into your business. Think of good sleep as the time when you turn on your inner magnet. Wake up rested and in a great mood because of your Life S.A.V.E.R.S., and you'll attract more business because a happy entrepreneur is also a rich one.

The True Benefits of Sleep

You may not realize how powerful sleep actually is. While you're happily wandering through your dreams, sleep is doing some hard work on your behalf and delivering a host of amazing benefits.

Improve your memory. Your mind is surprisingly busy while you snooze. During sleep you clean out damaging toxins that are by-products of brain function during the day, strengthen memories, and practice skills learned while you were awake through a process called consolidation.

"If you are trying to learn something, whether it's physical or mental, you learn it to a certain point with practice," says Dr. David Rapoport, who is an associate professor at NYU Langone Medical Center and a sleep expert, "but something happens while you sleep that makes you learn it better."

In other words, if you're trying to learn something new, whether it's Spanish, a new tennis swing, or the specifications of a new product in your arsenal, you'll perform better when you get adequate sleep.

Live longer. Too much or too little sleep is associated with a shorter life span, although it's not clear if it's a cause or an effect. In a 2010 study of women ages 50-79, more deaths occurred in women who got fewer than five hours or more than six-and-a-half hours of sleep per night. Getting the right amount of sleep is a good idea for your long-term health.

Be more creative. While sleep improves memory and learning, REM sleep in particular seems to boost your ability to solve problems creatively. Researchers from Harvard studied sleepers before and after naps. For control, they put other participants through the same battery of questions without a nap. Some of the sleeping participants were allowed to slip into REM sleep while others were denied the pleasure. Nappers who slept more deeply enhanced their creative problem solving performance by nearly 40 percent when compared to their counterparts who slept for less time and those who didn't.

Attain and maintain a healthy weight more easily. If you're over-weight, you won't have the same energy levels as those at a healthy weight. Along with changing your lifestyle to include more exercise and diet changes with your Miracle Morning practice and Energy Engineering, you'll want to plan an earlier bedtime. Putting addi-tional physical demands on your body means you will need to counter balance those demands with plenty of rest.

Researchers with the University of Chicago found that diet-ers who were well-rested lost more fat—up to 56 percent more—than those who were sleep deprived, who lost more muscle mass. Participants' hunger actually increased when they lacked sufficient shut-eye. The key connection between sleep and metabolism is their brain connection: the same sectors of the brain control both func-tions. Hormones that happen to increase your appetite are released when you don't get enough sleep.

Feel less stressed. This probably isn't news to you: A good night's rest reduces your stress. Diminished sleep and stress affect car-diovascular health to further impact your long-term health and short-term energy supply. Along with cutting your stress, your commitment to sleep allows the body to better control blood pressure. It is also believed that sleep affects cholesterol levels, which play a significant role in heart disease.

Avoid mistakes and accidents. The National Highway Traffic Safe-ty Administration reports that fatigue is responsible for most "fatal, single-car, run-off-the-road crashes due to the driver's performance." What's more shocking is that driver fatigue is cited in these crashes more often than alcohol! This is because lack of sleep affects reaction time and decision-making, which is a dangerous combination on the road.

If insufficient sleep for only one night can be as detrimental to your driving ability as having an alcoholic drink, imagine how it af-fects your ability to maintain the focus necessary to become a top entrepreneur.

So, how many hours of sleep do you *really* need? Only you truly know how much sleep you need to hit home run after home run. If you struggle with falling or staying asleep, and it is a concern for you, I highly recommend reading Shawn Stevenson's book, *Sleep Smarter: 21 Proven Tips to Sleep Your Way to a Better Body, Better Health, and Bigger Success*. It's one of the best written and most researched books that I've seen on the topic of sleep.

Getting consistent and effective rest is as critical to performing at your best as what you eat. A good night's sleep provides the basis for a day of clear thought, sustained energy, peak performance, and maximum creativity for the problems that arise during the day. Commit to getting enough sleep with a consistent bedtime because what may be even more important than how many hours of sleep you get each night is how you approach the act of waking up in the morning.

How Much Sleep Do We Really Need?

The first thing some experts will tell you about how many hours of sleep we need is that there is no universal number. The ideal length of nighttime sleep varies among people, and is influenced by factors such as age, genetics, stress, overall health, how much exercise a person gets, our diet—including how late we consumed our last meal—and countless other factors.

For example, if your diet consists of fast food, processed foods, excessive sugar, etc., then your body will be challenged to recharge and rejuvenate while you sleep. It will work long into the night to detoxify and filter out the poisons that you've put into it. When you eat a clean diet of living food, as we covered in the last section, then your body will rest more easily. The person who eats a clean diet will almost always wake up feeling refreshed, have more energy, and be able to function optimally, even if she gets *less* sleep than the person who eats poorly.

Since there is such a wide variety of opposing evidence from countless studies and experts, and since the amount of sleep needed varies from person to person, I'm not going to attempt to make a case that there is one *right* approach to sleep. Instead, I'll share my own real-world results, from personal experience and experimentation, and from studying the sleep habits of some of the greatest minds in history. I'll warn you, some of this may be somewhat controversial.

How To Wake Up With More Energy (On Less Sleep)

Through experimenting with various sleep durations—as well as learning those of many other Miracle Morning practitioners, who have tested this theory—Hal found that how our sleep affects our biology is largely affected by our own personal *belief* about how much sleep we need. In other words, how we feel when we wake up in the morning—and this is a very important distinction—is not solely based on how many hours of sleep we got, but significantly influenced by what we told ourselves we were going to feel when we woke up.

For example, if you *believe* that you need eight hours of sleep to feel rested, but you're getting into bed at midnight and have to wake up at 6:00 a.m., you're likely to tell yourself, "I'm going to feel exhausted in the morning." Then, what happens as soon as your alarm clock goes off, you open your eyes, and realize it's time to wake up? What's the first thought that you think? It's the same thought you had before bed! "Geez, I only got six hours of sleep. I feel exhausted." It's a self-fulfilling, self-sabotaging prophecy. If you tell yourself you're going to feel tired in the morning, then you are absolutely going to feel tired. If you believe that you need eight hours to feel fully rested, then you're not going to feel rested on anything less. But what if you changed your beliefs?

The mind-body connection is a powerful thing, and I believe we must take responsibility for every aspect of our lives, including the power to wake up every day feeling energized, regardless of how many hours of sleep we get.

You Snooze, You Lose: The Truth About Waking Up

The old saying, "you snooze, you lose" has a much deeper meaning than any of us realized. When you hit the snooze button and delay waking up until you *must*—meaning you wait to until the time when you have to be somewhere, do something, or take care of someone else—consider that you're starting your day with resistance. Every time you hit the snooze button, you're in a state of resistance to your day, to your life, and to waking up and creating the life you say you want.

According to Robert S. Rosenberg, medical director of the Sleep Disorders Centers of Prescott Valley and Flagstaff, Arizona, "When you hit the snooze button repeatedly, you're doing two negative things to yourself. First, you're fragmenting what little extra sleep you're getting so it is of poor quality. Second, you're starting to put yourself through a new sleep cycle that you aren't giving yourself enough time to finish. This can result in persistent grogginess throughout the day."

If you're not already, make sure you start following the Five-Step, Snooze-Proof, Wake-Up Strategy in chapter 2, and you'll be poised to win. If getting to bed on time is your challenge, try setting a "bedtime alarm" that sounds an hour before your ideal bedtime, prompting you to start winding down so you can hit the sack. This will give you an advantage when it comes time to rise and shine, the time when you can set yourself up to make the most of your day.

When you wake up each day with passion and purpose, you join the small percentage of high achievers who are living their dreams. Most importantly, you will be happy. By simply changing your approach to waking up in the morning, you will change everything. But don't take my word for it—trust these famous early risers: Oprah Winfrey, Tony Robbins, Bill Gates, Howard Schultz, Deepak Chopra, Wayne Dyer, Thomas Jefferson, Benjamin Franklin, Albert Einstein, Aristotle, and far too many more to list here.

No one ever taught us that by learning how to consciously set our intention to wake up each morning with a genuine desire—even enthusiasm—to do so, we can change our entire lives.

If you're snoozing each morning until the last possible moment when you have to head into the work of your day and then coming home and zoning out in front of the television until you go to bed (this used to be my daily routine), I've got to ask you this: *When are you going to develop yourself into the person you need to be to create the levels of health, wealth, happiness, success, and freedom that you truly want and deserve? When are you going to live your life instead of numbly going through the motions looking for every possible distraction to escape reality? What if your reality—your life—could finally be something that you can't wait to be conscious for? And what if that all starts with how you wake up?*

There is no better day than today for you to give up who you've been for who you can become and upgrade the life you've been living for the one you really want. There is no better book than the one you are holding in your hands to show you how to become the person you need to be who is capable of quickly attracting, creating and sustaining the life you have always wanted.

3. Rest to Recharge

The conscious counterpart to sleep is *rest*. While some people use the terms interchangeably, they're really quite different. You might get eight hours of sleep, but if you spend all your waking hours on the go, then you won't have time to think or recharge your physical, mental, and emotional batteries. When you work all day, run from activity to activity after hours, and then finish with a quick dinner and late bedtime, you don't allow for a period of rest.

Likewise, spending weekends taking the kids to soccer, volleyball, or basketball then heading out to see a football game, going to church, singing in the choir, attending several birthday parties, etc., can do more harm than good. While each of these activities is great, maintaining a fully packed schedule doesn't allow for time to recharge.

We live in a culture that perpetuates the belief that when our days are busy and exciting, we are more valuable, more important, or more alive. In truth, we are all those things when we can be at peace within our own skin. Despite our best intentions to live balanced lives, the modern world demands that we are almost always connected and productive, and these demands can drain us emotionally, spiritually, and physically.

What if, instead of being constantly on the go, you valued intentional quiet time, sacred space, and periods of purposeful silence? How might that improve your life, your physical and emotional well-being, and your ability to achieve entrepreneurial success?

It may seem counterintuitive to take time out when your to-do list is a mile long, but the fact is that more rest is a prerequisite to truly productive work.

Research proves that rest melts your stress away. Practices like yoga and meditation also lower your heart rate, blood pressure, and oxygen consumption. They alleviate hypertension, arthritis, insomnia, depression, infertility, cancer, and anxiety. The spiritual benefits of resting are profound. Slowing down and getting quiet means you can actually hear the wisdom and knowledge of your inner voice. Rest and its close sibling, relaxation, allow us to reconnect with the world in and around us, inviting ease in our lives and a sense of contentment.

And yes, in case you're wondering, you'll be more productive, nicer to your friends and family members (not to mention your employees and clients), and in general much happier as well. When we rest, it's like letting the earth lie fallow rather than constantly planting and harvesting. Our personal batteries need to be recharged. The best way to recharge them is to truly and simply rest.

Easy Ways to Rest

Most of us confuse rest with recreation. To rest, we do things like hike, garden, work out, or even party. Any of these activities can only be termed restful because they are breaks from work, but truthfully they are not, and cannot, be defined as rest.

Rest has been defined as a kind of waking sleep experienced while you are alert and aware. Rest is the essential bridge to sleep, and we achieve rest and sleep the same way: by making space for and allowing it to happen. Every living organism needs rest, including you. When we don't take the time to rest, eventually its absence takes a toll on the body.

- If you are now investing five or more minutes each morning during your Life S.A.V.E.R.S. to meditate or sit in silence, that is a great start.

- You can reserve one day of the week for rest. You can read, watch a movie, do something low-key with family, or even spend time alone. Try cooking at home, playing board games with your kids, and enjoying each other's company.

- When you're driving, drive in silence: turn off the radio and stow your phone.

- Go for a walk without your earbuds in. Time in nature without intention or goals, such as burning calories, can feel like rest.

- Turn off the television. Designate a half hour, an hour, or even half a day for silence.

- Try taking regular conscious breaths during which you focus on the inhale and exhale or the space between breaths.

- You can also mindfully drink a cup of tea, read something inspirational, write in your journal, take a hot bath, or get a massage.

- Attend a retreat. It could be with your team, a group of friends, your church, any community with which you are involved, family, your spouse, or on your own in nature.

Even taking a nap is a powerful way to rest and recharge. If I'm feeling drained during the day for some reason and still have a long day ahead, I won't hesitate to hit the reset button with a 20 or 30-minute power nap. Napping also can lead to better sleep patterns.

It's helpful to set a specific time for rest. Put boundaries around it so you can claim that time.

The Rest Habit

As an entrepreneur, you're in the trenches by default. You'll need to schedule your time for rest and self-care in the same way you schedule the other appointments in your life. The energy you get back will reward you many times over.

Rest certainly isn't something we were taught in school, and it may not come to you naturally at first. After all, you're a driven, hard-charging entrepreneur. So, you may find that you need to be conscious about making it a priority. Learning different mindfulness practices and bringing them into your everyday life is an effective way to deeply rest your body, mind, and spirit. Practices, such as midday meditation, yoga, and purposeful silence, are powerful ways to go within and achieve restful states of being, particularly when you commit to practicing them regularly.

The more you integrate periods of rest and silence into your daily life, the bigger the payoff will be. During more tranquil periods, perhaps you won't need to rest as much, but periods of intensity (such as meeting a huge quota or a big deadline) may require more rest and silence than usual.

Combining exercise, healthy food choices, consistent sleep, and rest will give you a quantum leap in the right direction for you and your business. Keep in mind that when you try to adopt these three practices—to eat, sleep, and rest more effectively—you may at first find the process uncomfortable. You may encounter some resistance. Counteract the urge to run from the discomfort by making a commitment to begin putting them into practice today.

Putting Energy Engineering into Action

Step One: Commit to eating and drinking for energy by prioritizing the energy consequences of the foods you eat above the taste. After your initial glass of water in the morning, ingest some form of healthy fat to fuel your brain. Try incorporating one new healthy meal of living foods in your diet each day. Instead of snacking on potato chips, try kale chips or fresh organic fruit. And remember to keep water with you at all times so that you stay hydrated.

Step Two: Sleep and wake to win by choosing a consistent daily bedtime *and* wake up time. Based on the time you rise for your Miracle Morning, back your way into a bedtime that ensures that you will get enough sleep. Maintain a specific bedtime for a few weeks to get your body acclimated. If you need a little nudge to get to bed on time, set an alarm that prompts you to start winding down one hour before bedtime. After a couple of weeks, feel free to play with the number of hours you leave for sleeping to optimize your energy levels.

Step Three: Incorporate time into your daily calendar to rest and recharge. Whether that's meditation, a nap, going for a walk, or doing an activity that brings you joy. Hal takes a two-hour lunch break every day, which gives him time to play basketball or wakeboard—two activities that he loves to do and that thoroughly re-energize him. What activities can you plan for your day that will re-energize you? In addition to your Miracle Morning routine, schedule regular daily periods to rest and recharge.

Entrepreneur Profile

Jayson Gaignard

Jayson Gaignard's company is MastermindTalks.

Top Business Accomplishments

❖ Jayson has been named one of the Top Networkers to Watch by *Forbes*.

❖ He is the founder of one of the most exclusive entrepreneurial communities in the world (which has an acceptance rate lower than Harvard University).

Morning Routine

❖ Before bed, Jayson plans the three top things that he needs to accomplish the following day and prioritizes one of them above all others. This helps him avoid decision fatigue.

❖ Because sleep is important to him, he goes to bed by 9:30 p.m.

❖ He wakes up at 5:00 a.m.

❖ Then he writes or brainstorms in two 25-minute sessions or pomodoros.

❖ He stays fully disconnected from email and social media in the morning to reserve that time for deep creative work.

❖ Jayson focuses on his top priority for two or three pomodoros. He has the most willpower first thing in the morning, so it's best for him to work on the most challenging stuff first.

❖ He does a simple, quick workout and stretches to get his blood flowing.

❖ Then he does five minutes of open-eyed meditation.

❖ He has found a lot of information surrounding the medical benefits to cold thermogenesis, so he takes a cold shower next.

❖ By the time his daughter is awake, he is ready for the second part of his day.

— 6 —

ENTREPRENEUR ELEVATION SKILL #3:

UNWAVERING FOCUS

The successful warrior is the average man, with laser-like focus.
–BRUCE LEE, World-Renowned
Martial Artist and Actor

We've all met that person. You know—*that* person. The one who runs marathons, coaches little league, volunteers at her son's school lunch program, and maybe writes a novel on the side. And on top of all that? She's an incredible entrepreneur, getting tons of press, winning awards, and knocking it out of the park when it comes to growing her business, year after year. I bet you know someone like that—someone who seems unexplainably productive.

Or maybe you know *this* person—the entrepreneur who runs a million-dollar plus business, but never seems to be working in it. He's always playing golf or out on the lake in the middle of the workweek.

When you see him, he's talking about the vacation he just returned from or the one he's getting ready to leave for. He's fit, happy, and makes every person he comes in contact with feel like a million bucks.

What you might not realize, though, is exactly how people like this do it. Maybe you thought they were lucky. Or gifted. Or connected. Or had the right personality. Or was born with superpowers!

While those things could help when it comes to entrepreneurship, I know from experience that the real superpower behind every unbelievably productive entrepreneur is *unwavering focus*. Unwavering focus is the ability to maintain clarity about your highest priorities, take all the energy you've learned to generate for yourself, channel it into the crucial activities that matter most, and keep it there—regardless of what is going on around you or how you feel in the moment. This ability is key to becoming an exceptional entrepreneur.

One crucial role of an entrepreneur is to provide a vision for the organization that will be shared internally and externally to keep everyone working in unison to co-create your predetermined future. That is the purpose of the Vivid Vision, which I'll cover in detail in the next chapter. It is a tool designed to allow entrepreneurs to look three years into the future, to where the business should be, and then work backward to achieve the aspiration with annual goals.

Developing and maintaining that vision demands the unwavering focus on the big-picture issues that occur within the market, industry, and society at large. Like a captain piloting a ship across the ocean (prior to the advent of GPS, for the sake of the analogy), the CEO must chart the best course and trust that the first mate will see to it that the vessel is in shipshape, the crew is doing its job, and the passengers well attended.

If you are constantly dealing with the disruption of email, phone calls, meetings, face time, hiring and firing, and various other forms of minutiae, then your focus is downward when it should be forward.

When you harness the power of focus, you don't become superhuman, but you can achieve seemingly superhuman results. The reasons for this are surprisingly straightforward.

- **Unwavering Focus makes you more effective.** Being effective doesn't mean to do the most things or to do things the fastest. It means to do the *right* things. You engage in the activities that create forward momentum in your company and generate sales.

- **Unwavering Focus makes you more efficient.** Being efficient means achieving what you need to achieve with the fewest resources, such as time, energy, or money. Every time your mind wanders away from your work, you waste those things—particularly time. In entrepreneurship, time is money, so every moment that your focus wavers is another dollar (or hundreds of thousands of dollars) lost.

- **Unwavering Focus makes you productive.** Understand that, just because you're *busy* doesn't mean you're *productive*. In fact, broke entrepreneurs are usually the busiest. When you have a clear vision, identify your highest priorities, and consistently execute your most leveraged activities, you'll go from being busy to being productive. Too often we confuse being busy—engaged in activities that don't produce results —like checking emails or cleaning your car or reorganizing your to-do list for the twelfth time this month—with being productive.

By taking the steps that I'm about to reveal, you'll learn how to develop the habit of unwavering focus and join the ranks of the most productive entrepreneurs in the world.

If you combine those benefits, you will perform at a peak level and earn a *lot* more. Perhaps the greatest value of focus, however, is that it moves the needle not just in terms of your bottom line, but also in every important area of your life. Rather than scattering your energy across multiple areas and getting mediocre results across the board, focus releases your untapped selling potential *and* improves your life.

Now let's turn your Miracle Morning to the task. Here are four steps you need to add, in addition to your Miracle Morning, for sustained focus.

1. Find Your Best Environment(s) for Unwavering Focus

Let's start here: *You need an environment that supports your commitment to unwavering focus.* It might be your office, home office, or it could be a coffee shop. No matter how modest, though, you need a place where you go to focus on conducting business.

Part of the reason for this is simple logistics. If your work is scattered from the trunk of your car to the kitchen counter, you simply can't be effective. A bigger reason, however, is that having a place where you focus triggers the habit of focusing. Trying to work at your kitchen table or make prospecting calls while sitting on your living room couch leaves you susceptible to being pulled into unproductive activities, like grabbing a bite to eat or watching television. Sit at the same desk to do great work at the same time every day, and soon, you'll find yourself slipping into the zone just by sitting down in that place.

If you're on the road a lot, like me, then your car, your suitcase, your hotel room and possibly airports, hotel lobbies, or random coffee shops are part of your focus space too. Build habits for how you pack and work on the road, and you can trigger great focus the same way you do at the office. When you are prepared and always have with you exactly what you need, you can work anywhere. I could even come and work on your couch or in your guestroom if necessary.

2. Clear the Unfocused Clutter

Clutter is a focus killer, and it's our next stop on the journey. There is a reason why Marie Kondo's book, *The Life-Changing Magic of Tidying Up* is one of the best-selling nonfiction books of the last decade. You will inspire a calm, motivated mindset when you declutter both your physical and mental space.

Which brings me to my next point. There are two kinds of clutter, mental and physical, and we all have them both. We carry thoughts in our minds about tasks that need to be done, like these: *My sister's birthday is coming up. I have to get her a gift and card. I had a great time at dinner the other night. I need to send the host a thank-you note. I have to answer the email from my new client before I leave the office today.*

Then there are the physical items we accumulate. Stacks of paper. Old magazines. Sticky notes. Clothes we never wear. The pile of junk in the garage. The trinkets, knickknacks, and tokens that collect as we go through life.

Clutter of either type creates the equivalent of a heavy fog, and to become focused, you need to be able to *see*. To clear your vision, you'll want to get those mental items out of your head and gathered in a safe place so you can relieve the mental stress of trying to remember them. And then, you'll want to get the physical items out of your way.

Here's a simple process to help you clear the fog and create the clarity you need to focus.

- **Create a master to-do list**. You probably have lots of things that haven't been written down yet. Start with those. And all those tiny little sticky notes that clutter your desk, computer screen, planner, countertops, refrigerator … Are there other places? Put those notes and action items on your master list in one place, whether that's a physical journal or a list on your phone, so you can completely clear your mental storage. Feeling better? Keep going! We're just getting started.

- **Purge your workspace**. Schedule a half (or full) day to go through every stack of paper, file folder stuffed with documents, and tray full of unopened mail in your office. You get the gist. Throw out or shred what you don't need. Scan or file what matters. Make note of any items that need attention and cannot be delegated in your journal. Then pick a time in your schedule to complete them.

- **Declutter your life.** Whenever possible, clean up and clear out every drawer, closet, cabinet, and trunk that doesn't give you a sense of calm and peace when you see it. This includes your car. This might take a few hours or a few days. Schedule a short time each day until everything is complete. Saying, "I just need a weekend to declutter," is a sure way to never start. Pick a single drawer and start there. You'll be surprised at how the small bursts of work will make a big difference in your environment. Try S.J. Scott and Barrie Davenport's book,

10-Minute Declutter: The Stress-Free Habit for Simplifying Your Home for help with this process.

Getting physically and mentally organized will allow you to focus at a level you would never believe possible. It leaves your energy nowhere to go except to what matters.

3. Protect Yourself from Interruptions

In addition to my coaching and speaking business, I lead the COO Alliance (a mastermind group), and have authored four books. I'm married and have two children. As you can imagine, my time is critically important to me, just as I'm sure yours is to you.

To avoid distraction and ensure that my attention is focused on the task at hand, my phone is almost always set on *Do Not Disturb* mode. This blocks all incoming calls, texts, or notifications from email and social media. This is a simple thing that dramatically increases my daily productivity and ability to remain focused on the task in front of me. I recommend returning phone calls and emails at predesignated times, according to your time-blocked schedule, not when someone happens to contact you.

You can apply the same philosophy and strategies to any notifications or alerts as well as your availability for colleagues, employees, and even clients. *Do Not Disturb* isn't only a setting on your phone. Let your team know when you're available and when they need to leave you undisturbed.

4. Build a Foundation for Unwavering Focus

Once you identify your best environment and begin the process of decluttering your life, you should experience a remarkable increase in focus simply from clearing the fog in your mind.

Now, it's time to take things to the next level. I use three questions to improve my focus every day. They are:

- What's working that I should *keep doing* (or do more of)?

- What do I need to *start doing* to accelerate results?

- What do I need to immediately *stop doing* that's holding me back from going to the next level?

If you can answer those three questions and take action on the answers, you'll discover a whole new level of productivity you probably didn't think was possible. Let's look at each question in detail.

What Do You Need to Keep Doing (or Do More of)?

Let's face it, not all entrepreneurial tactics and strategies are created equal. Some work better than others. Some work for a while and then become less effective. Some even make things worse.

Right now, you're probably doing a lot of the right activities, and you'll be nodding right along as you read the coming chapters on the entrepreneurial elevation principles. If you already know the things you're doing that are working, jot those down. Perhaps you're constantly finding potential customers and closing deals, for example. Put that on the "what's working" list. Perhaps having your COO attend the COO Alliance is helping—add that to the list too.

Make sure you choose things that are actually contributing to increasing your business. It's easy to keep the things you *like* doing, but this is entrepreneurship—you need to make sure that the activities you're doing are directly related to producing new revenue, identifying and hiring new employees, and, ultimately, putting money in your bank account. Consider the 80/20 Rule (originally the Pareto principle), which shows that roughly 80 percent of our results come from 20 percent of our efforts. Which 20 percent of your activities impact 80 percent of your results?

Capture the activities that are working in your journal. (Among them, I hope, will be that you've started doing the Life S.A.V.E.R.S.) Everything that's on that list is a keep doing until it's replaced by something even more effective.

For all the "keep doing" activities on your list, make sure you're completely honest with yourself about *what you need to be doing more of* (in other words, what you're currently not doing enough of). Remember, any percentage that you increase an identified best process, over an extended time, should result in that same percentage of an increase in the growth of your business overall. Go from 20 to 30 calls a day (a 50 percent increase), and it's only a matter of time before you'll see your business increase by roughly 50 percent, and much more as your employees begin to duplicate your level of effectiveness.

Keep doing what's working, and depending on how much more you want to sell or grow, simply do *more* of what's working.

What Do You Need to Start Doing?

Once you've captured what's working—and determined what's working that you need to do more of—it's time to decide what *else* you can do to accelerate your success.

I have a few top-shelf suggestions to prime the pump and get you started.

- Organize your database for targeted follow up with prospective clients as well as your sphere of influence. For comprehensive training on this topic, I highly recommend Michael J. Maher's best-selling book *The 7 Levels of Communication.*

Make sure your online presence is driving business. You can either use a service, such as *Likeable Hub* (https://likeablehub.com), or hire someone to optimize your social media accounts and improve SEO, conversion rates, and content development.

Create your *Foundational Schedule*—Develop your recurring, ideal weekly schedule with a time-blocked calendar, as I discussed in chapter 4 so that, every day when you wake up, your highest priorities are already predetermined and planned. Then make any necessary adjustments on Sunday night for the following week.

Have whatever tools and materials you might need on hand at all times. Be sure to stock and restock so you are always prepared to do what needs to get done.

- Once you've identified the activities you're spending time on that do *not* directly impact your growth (in other words, the tasks that are important but that you shouldn't be doing), plan your first (or next) hire. This could be a personal assistant, a virtual assistant, an intern, or even someone new to the business who is eager to spend time with you and can help out. Realize that hiring someone to free up your time is an *investment*, not an expense. What would it be worth for you to free up enough of your time to increase your sales by 20–50 percent? It's time for you to start thinking bigger. If you don't have an assistant, you are one.

I caution you not to become overwhelmed here. Keep in mind that Rome wasn't built in a day. You don't need to identify 58 action items and implement them right away. The great news about having a daily scribing, or journaling, practice means that you can capture everything. Then, one or two at a time, add them to your success arsenal until they become habits.

What Do You Need to Stop Doing?

By now you've most likely added a few items to start doing. If you're wondering where the time is going to come from, this might be your favorite step of all. It's time to let go of some of the things you've been doing up until now that don't serve you to make room for the ones that do.

I'm fairly sure there are a number of daily activities you will be relieved to stop doing, thankful to delegate to someone else, or grateful to release.

Why not stop

- eating unhealthy, energy-draining foods that suck the life and motivation out of you?
- working when you're tired and on the weekends and holidays?
- replying to texts and emails instantly?
- answering the phone? (Let it go to voicemail and reply when the timing works best for you.)
- doing repetitive tasks such as paying the bills, buying groceries several times a week, or even cleaning your house?

Or, if you want to improve your focus in one simple step, try this easy fix:

Stop responding to buzzes and sounds like a trained seal.

Do you really need to be notified when you receive texts, emails, and social media notifications? Nope, didn't think so. Go into the settings of your phone, tablet, and computer and turn all of your notifications *off*.

Technology exists for your benefit, and you can take control of it this very minute. How often you check your phone messages, texts, and email can and should be directed by *you*. Let's face it, we're entrepreneurs, not emergency room physicians. We don't need to be accessible and instantly responding to others 24/7/365. An effective alternative is scheduling times throughout the day to check in on what's happening, what needs your immediate attention, what items can be added to your schedule or master to-do list, and what can be deleted, ignored, or forgotten.

Your voicemail message can let people know you will check it at noon and 4:00 p.m. daily. If their call is an emergency, they can, and should, text you at the same number. I use Grasshopper.com to assist me with my voice mail. By setting proper expectations around response times, prospects, customers, and team members will never be disappointed when it takes you a few hours to get back to them.

Unwavering Focus Is a Habit

Focus is like a muscle that you build over time. And, like a muscle, you need to show up and do the work to make it grow. Cut yourself some slack if you falter, but keep pushing forward. It will get easier. It might take you time to learn to focus, but every day that you try, you'll continue to get better at it. Ultimately, this is about *becoming* someone who focuses, which starts with seeing yourself as such. I recommend that you add a few lines to your affirmations about your commitment to unwavering focus and what you will do each day to develop it.

Most entrepreneurs would be shocked to discover just how little time they spend on truly important activities relevant to business growth each day. Today, or in the next 24 hours, schedule 60 minutes to focus on the *single most important business growth task you do*, and you'll be amazed not only by your productivity, but also by how empowering it feels.

By now, you've added some pretty incredible action items and focus areas to your success arsenal. After you complete the steps below, head into the next section where we will sharpen your entrepreneurial skills and combine them with the Life S.A.V.E.R.S. in ways you might not have heard or thought of before!

Putting Unwavering Focus into Action

Step One: Choose or create your ideal environment to support unwavering focus. If your focus is optimum when you're working in a public place, such as a coffee shop, schedule focused time blocks at Starbuck's. If you work from home, make sure you've implemented step two, below.

Step Two: Clear your physical and mental clutter. Start by scheduling a half-day to clean up your workspace. Then, clear your mind with a brain dump. Unload all those little to-do lists floating around in your head. Create a master to-do list, either on your computer, in your phone, or in your journal.

Step Three: Protect yourself from interruptions that come from you and others. Limit distractions that might pull you away from your intended tasks. Turn off notifications, put your phone in Do Not Disturb mode, and set the expectation within your circle of influence that you are unavailable during focused time blocks but will get back to them during predesignated times.

Step Four: Start building your unwavering focus lists. Pull out your journal, or open a document or note on your phone or computer, and create the following three lists:

- **What do I need to keep doing (or do more of)?**
- **What do I need to start doing?**
- **What do I need to stop doing?**

Begin jotting down everything that comes to mind. Review your lists and determine which activities can be automated, outsourced, or delegated. Consider how much time you spend on your top business growth and income-producing activities. Repeat this process until you are clear on what your process is. Then start time blocking your days so that you spend close to 80 percent of your time on tasks that produce results. Delegate the rest.

How I Stay Focused

One thing I like to do to keep my focus positive is to make a list of all the things I have accomplished during the week. It's an act of self-congratulations, which serves as a moment to pause, take stock, and realize that progress is steadily being made toward the intended result. It's also a way to keep your chin up when times get rough, a way of avoiding burnout and a reminder that you can and are doing the things you set out to do. Don't go negative, it's futile. Learn from your mistakes and keep your attitude positive. If I set five new goals for myself for next week, I will also write down five things I accomplished in this past week so I feel great about my efforts. I know this will help create more positive momentum.

This form of positive focus is so effective that I've begun something similar with the entrepreneurs I coach. I tell them that, any time they set a new goal, they should simultaneously praise or reward themselves for something they have already accomplished. Setting a weekly goal? Pat yourself on the back for a goal you achieved the prior week. A quarterly project you are setting out to do? Take a moment to reflect on the last quarterly project you finished.

This idea goes back to the balance inherent in yin and yang. Opposites *can be* complementary and create harmony (the right type of opposites, that is). It's easy for us to get caught up in the idea of pursuing ever greater goals and conquering the next mountain. We hold the false belief that if we can only reach that next mountain, we'll be happy. The reality for the entrepreneur is that there will always be another mountain we want to climb. So it's vital that we enjoy the journey.

Another way I stay focused is to put my phone away at night. I put mine in the kitchen or my office when I got to bed. The last thing I need is access to a time-sucking device during my crucial recovery hours. Furthermore, first thing in the morning is not the time to delve into the day's obstacle course. Ease into it *after* you've done your Life S.A.V.E.R.S., taken a hot shower, poured a cup of coffee, and settled into your morning. If you can put it off until after breakfast, even better.

If that's difficult for you, consider a habit-forming app to get used to this new routine. I use an app called Way of Life, which allows me to select the habits I want to incorporate and check them off as I do them each day. One of my habits that I track is "Life S.A.V.E.R.S. Before Phone." It serves as a reminder and, in its own way, a form of accountability.

Finally, to keep my focus, I invest heavily in myself. What I mean is that when I go to events, conferences, or join a new group, I surround myself with people who are really smart and who are doing cool stuff. That focuses me. If I'm the smartest guy in the room, I'm in the wrong room. In the past few years, I have joined and heavily participated in some new groups for high growth entrepreneurs: Genius Network, Mastermind Talks, Strategic Coach, and Maverick. These are networks of incredibly driven, focused entrepreneurs who continually have been focused on helping me raise my game as well.

I agree with Jim Rohn when he says, "You are the average of the five people you spend most of your time with." Who do you spend your time with? If you invest your time and money in high-performing individuals, you will make far more money than you ever could playing the stock market. Think of it this way: Your *network* is your *net worth*.

Of course, investing in oneself goes beyond surrounding yourself with other people. I listen to podcasts while I run, which allows me to maximize my time and accomplish two things that are important to my well-being at the same time. I also listen to audiobooks this way, which allows me to spend quality time at home with my family, rather than disconnected from them while I read in private.

Consider the Five F's, categories that cover major areas of life: friends, family, fitness, finance and faith. Ideally, we could maintain a balance of these foundational pillars at all times, keeping them in perfect harmony. But that's not the way the world works. At best, you might adequately manage two or three at a time, while the others suffer. There will be times you are able to focus your attention on friends and family, during a vacation, for instance. At other times, they will take a back seat, say, to your faith and finances, perhaps as you pray for a VC to fund your startup.

Here are some tips that have always worked for me:

1. Keep your Vivid Vision and Annual and Quarterly Goals Top of Mind

Write down your Vivid Vision and goals, share them with others, and reread them regularly will help you focus and take action to move toward them. You can select the key projects to work on and say no to other projects that are only busy work. (More on the Vivid Vision in the next chapter.)

2. Focus on Two to Three important tasks per day

Yes, we all have an infinite number of things that need to be done. But it's about working on the critical few things versus the important many.

3. Start Your Day with Your Top Three Tasks

To make sure you get those three completed, do them early. As soon as you start working, dive into these critical tasks. The email can wait. In fact, sometimes the most productive work you'll do will be before leaving the house for your office. That way you're working on the top three tasks before you get distracted by email and other activities.

4. Work in Bite-Size Chunks

Try not to focus on the whole goal or project. Instead zero in on smaller parts and get it done in chunks. There is an old saying that the best way to eat an elephant is one bite at a time.

By focusing on the smaller parts, you won't get discouraged because the goal is too big. You're less likely to become distracted by day dreaming about the big goal either. Here are a few examples:

- Writing two blog posts a day
- Make three sales calls a day
- Call three customers a day

Those bite-size chunks will lead to strong social media marketing, more landed clients, and more insights into your customer service. And they are easy to complete.

5. Visualize Yourself Working

See yourself being focused and getting the work done. Feel yourself pounding through it. And then you'll suddenly get into the groove. Visualization has been proving to work the same parts of the mind as actually doing the activity.

6. Get away from distractions

Get away from anything that distracts you. Don't sit near a TV. Move away from employees or kids who are talking. Work early in the morning before everyone comes into the office. Work off site from a club or meeting space. Work from your back yard. I routinely took Thursday mornings out of the office as focus days.

7. Pomodoro

Mentioned previously in this book, the Pomodoro Technique is a time management method developed in the late 1980s. The technique uses a timer to break work into intervals, traditionally 25 minutes in length, separated by short breaks. These intervals are named pomodoros, the plural in English of the Italian word pomodoro (tomato), after the tomato-shaped kitchen timer that the creator used as a university student. The method is based on the idea that frequent breaks can improve mental agility. I use an app on my iPhone called Focus Time to track mine.

There are six stages in the technique:

1. Decide on the task to be done.

2. Set the pomodoro timer (traditionally to 25 minutes).

3. Work on the task until the timer rings. If a distraction pops into your head, write it down, but immediately get back on task.

4. After the timer rings, put a check mark on a piece of paper.

5. If you have fewer than four check marks, take a short break (3–5 minutes), then go to step 1.

6. Otherwise (i.e., after four pomodoros) take a longer break (15–30 minutes), reset your check mark count to zero, then go to step 1.

Entrepreneur Profile

Joey Coleman

Joey Coleman's company is Design Symphony.

Top Business Accomplishments

❖ Joey is a top-rated speaker at many international and national speaking competitions with *New York Times* best-selling authors, celebrities, and internet sensations.

❖ He has helped several start-up clients achieve 7-8 figure exits.

❖ He's had an eclectic career, working for the US Secret Service, the White House, and the CIA; he practiced criminal defense law at a private firm; he taught professionals as part of an executive education program; and he started and ran a successful brand experience firm for over a decade.

❖ He has built and maintained an exciting portfolio of design and speaking clients including NASA, Zappos, the World Bank, the Save Darfur Coalition, Massachusetts Institute of Technology, Deloitte, YouTube, and Google.

❖ He has coached CEOs, professional speakers, and Olympic medalists in speaking and presenting skills

Morning Routine

❖ Joey wakes around 8:30 a.m.

❖ He scans Facebook.

❖ Then he writes in *The Five Minute Journal*.

- ❖ He showers and gets dressed while thinking about his intentions for the day and reviewing his schedule.

- ❖ Then he eats his morning meal, which consists of a nutrition bar, Berry Suja Juice, and 80 ounces of water.

- ❖ He spends time playing with his young sons.

- ❖ Later, he reviews the headlines of the day online.

- ❖ Then Joey goes through his email, clearing as many as possible in the course of an hour.

- ❖ Finally, he does his deep work on projects.

SECTION 3:

THE ENTREPRENEURIAL ELEVATION PRINCIPLES

— 7 —

ENTREPRENEUR ELEVATION PRINCIPLE #1:

CREATE A VIVID VISION

Whatever the mind can conceive and believe, the mind can achieve.

—NAPOLEON HILL

O ne of the most critical skills entrepreneurs needs to master is the ability to clarify and communicate their vision so everyone around them can see what they can see.

Many people create goals for the future, but most do not have a vision to go with them: they don't know what their life and business will look like when they achieve their goals. For example, if the goal is for revenue to triple or quadruple, what would that do to the company? How many people would need to be hired? Would you have to move your offices? Or would you need more than one l ocation? Would you provide different services? What might those look like? If creating a picture of your company is worth a thousand words, creating what I call a Vivid Vision™ of your company is worth even more.

Creating this Vivid Vision is the first step in doubling the size of your company. It may seem like a simple task, but experiencing that vision requires something more than looking at your business numbers. Most entrepreneurs discover that it requires a set of skills that differs significantly from those they normally use. In this chapter, I will show you how to develop these skills and create the Vivid Vision for your goals.

Before you devote time and energy to creating a vision of your company three years out, you must understand that it is not enough to create a Vivid Vision. Everyone in your organization must focus on the same Vivid Vision, and that Vivid Vision must be in sharp focus. If you and your employees are not all seeing the same vision of what your company will look and feel like three years hence, there is no chance it will happen the way you see it in your mind today.

Leaning out into the Future

Have you ever watched high jumpers right before a competition? The next time you watch the Olympic Games or the World Track and Field Championships, watch the high jumpers. Most of them stand still immediately before they start their run up to the bar. They close their eyes and often bob their heads up and down. They may even throw their heads backward as they focus their minds and see themselves running up to the bar and thrusting their bodies over it. Then they open their eyes, stare at the bar, and recreate in reality what they have just visualized. They use focus and visualization to achieve their desired results, and by imagining the obstacles they might face along the way, they prepare themselves mentally and physically for the challenge.

You should apply the focus and visualization techniques used by athletes to your business. If you and your employees aren't prepared—

in every way possible—to overcome the obstacles you might face on the path to your goals, you'll struggle to achieve them.

I first learned about this visualization process at a luncheon of the Young Entrepreneurs' Organization (now called Entrepreneurs' Organization, or EO) in 1998. At the time, I thought of this whole process as a way of leaning out into the future. Since then, I've heard other entrepreneurs describe visualization the same way. Obviously, it makes sense to others to think about the process this way.

Since that landmark luncheon, I've had the opportunity to learn more about the visualization process from an Olympic coach and sports psychologist. I have fine-tuned the technique through practice and had had enormous success using the visualization process in many business settings.

People respond to a challenge, and a Vivid Vision gives them that. When employees see what the company will look like three years out, they become clearer about what they can do to step up and add value to the company.

People find their work rewarding when they feel they are contributing toward a common vision. The Vivid Vision allows everyone in the company to feel as if they are a part of that bigger plan. And they can see with the same clarity what everyone else in the company, including the CEO, is seeing. Everyone senses they are on the same page—because they are.

When you have leaned out and grabbed hold of a clear vision for success, you're more likely to achieve your desired goal. That's why it's essential that you focus, develop your vision, and communicate to your employees, suppliers, shareholders, and even your clients what your business is going to look like at every stage of its growth. I'm not talking about a to-do list, a five-year plan, or a vision statement. Vision statements tend to get written by getting a group of people in a room pulling together the words that best describe their business. Then they create a one-sentence vision or mission statement for the company that no one cares about or reads ever again.

A Vivid Vision is so much more. A Vivid Vision comes about when an entrepreneur, founder, CEO—whatever you call yourself—

plants one foot in the present and then leans out and places the other foot in the future, in the territory of what could be.

I find three years to be the best period to use when creating a Vivid Vision. This timeline is short enough to be seen as realistic and achievable, yet long enough to allow you to realize innovative and expansive ideas. As a result, employees can incorporate the blueprint into their overarching and day-to-day goals, all the while enthusiastically striving for the picture of an even more successful future you have painted for them.

At the end of the process, your Vivid Vision will consist of a three- to four-page document that describes your vision for what your company will be three years out at double its present size. This may seem like an easy thing to produce, but it isn't.

How to Create Your Vivid Vision

The first step in creating a Vivid Vision is to start thinking about certain questions. When you peer into the future, what do you see? Don't worry about how you're going to build it. Focus on describing what you see over the next three years. One helpful exercise is to imagine that you're filming every aspect of your business: your employees, customers, supplier relationships, and so on. Play the film in your mind. What do the big picture and details look like three years out?

To answer the Vivid Vision questions, you'll need to free your mind from the day-to-day worries of running your business and allow yourself the freedom and concentration to visualize the future, just as Olympic athletes visualize their performances.

Here are a few steps to get you started on the right path. Although you are writing only three or four pages, they are among the most important pages you will ever write.

Get Out of Your office.

When you create a Vivid Vision for your company, you must leave your office. If you try to work anywhere in your building, whether sitting at your desk or in the boardroom, chances are you'll get dragged into the daily routine and won't allow your mind to wander into the future. When you work within your regular office, you will limit your mind with specific constraints, and that's the antithesis of this exercise. Forget current metrics, daily tasks, obligations, and the looming question of *how*. Simply let your mind wander.

The best way I've found to start a Vivid Vision is to get out in nature: sit by the ocean, go into a forest, find a spot in the mountains, or even lie down in a hammock in the backyard. I sketch and write, which is what I did when I wrote my company's Vivid Vision, the company I created to help entrepreneurs turn their dreams into reality.

Turn Off Your Computer

Don't use a computer to draft the initial Vivid Vision for your company. If you do, you could get sucked into the vortex of daily emails and tasks. Instead, put pen to paper. There is magic in writing it all out by hand first. I used a sketchpad of unlined paper. Initially, it was hard for me to think abstractly because I'm so left-brained. I turned the sketchpad sideways so it was in landscape mode and wrote my ideas about what my business would look like three years in the future.

Think WHERE—Not HOW

Look at the road in front of you. Don't focus on how you'll make it happen. When I was COO of 1-800-GOT-JUNK?, I purposefully never participated in creating the Vivid Vision because I was the *how* person. In contrast, the company's founder, Brian Scudamore, was the *where* person: He looked at the road ahead to see where he wanted the company to go. If I'd been involved in crafting the vision for the company, I'd have gotten in the way by constantly thinking about how we'd make it happen. Now I know how to get out of the way of progress and stop asking *how* all the time.

I like to use a technique called mind mapping, which isn't so much formal writing as it is jotting thoughts on paper to flesh out later. Mind mapping allows you to brainstorm without having to provide explanations or strategies for achieving the desired goal.

Step into Your Stretch Zone

It's a little hard for me to get creative, but not impossible. Creating a Vivid Vision requires you to step into your stretch zone, and I encourage you to do so. To ensure you're getting creative, think about crazy stuff—maybe something too outlandish to share at a meeting or even consider seriously. Here's a good rule of thumb to help you unleash your creativity: If what you think about during one of these sessions seems bizarre or unlikely, you should definitely include it in your Vivid Vision.

The Vivid Vision Checklist

Pretend you traveled in a time machine into the future. The date is December 31. Three years from now. You are walking around your company's offices with a clipboard in hand.

- What do you see?

- What do you hear?

- What do your clients say?

- What does the media write about you?

- What kind of comments are your employees making at the water cooler?

- What is the buzz about you in your community?

- What is your marketing like? Are you marketing your goods and services globally now? Are you launching new online and TV ads?

- How is the company running day to day? Is it organized and running like a clock?

- What kind of stuff do you do every day? Are you focused on strategy, team building, customer relationships, etc.?

- What do the company's financials reveal?

- How are you funded now?

- How are your core values being realized among your employees?

Include every area of your business: culture, staff, marketing, public relations, sales, IT, operations, finance, production, communication, customer service, engineering, values, employee engagement, work-life balance, etc. Cover interactions you'll have with stakeholders too. Remember that you are envisioning these aspects of your company after it has doubled in size.

Once I had put all the ideas in my head on paper, I was able to write a three-page description of what I had generated through mind mapping. I organized my descriptions by area.

Your Vivid Vision should be a written document, roughly three pages in length, that describes in detail what the company's highest-ranking executive envisions the company will look and feel like three years out, without detailing how the company will build or put the elements of the vision itself into place. It describes what the future looks like, not how you'll get there.

Enlist Support

When you finish your Vivid Vision, share it with your employees, suppliers, bankers, and lawyers. You'll then start to see people align with your goals, and the picture will become a reality.

It's incredibly beneficial for your employees, who will use your Vivid Vision as a means to understand their role in the grand scheme of things. I've even seen business areas within a company form their own version of a Vivid Vision that then dovetails with the overarching one. Overall, sharing your Vivid Vision with in-house people will prompt them to make decisions subconsciously that are in alignment with your blueprint. Then others outside the company with whom you share your Vivid Vision will also consciously help you make it happen because they see the employees are energized by the clarity of it as well.

Stick to a Three-Year Vivid Vision

The main reason to stick to the three-year timeline is that longer periods tend to feel overwhelming. Think of it this way: To create a Vivid Vision, you need to keep one foot firmly planted in the present while the other reaches out and taps tentatively on the soil of the future. If you go much further than three years ahead, you lose your balance and fall over. So, stay about three years out and write down what you see. Six months before the end of the three-year period, start crafting your next Vivid Vision.

Refer to Your Vivid Vision Often

Over time, your company's decision making will align with your Vivid Vision. I suggest having all your employees and suppliers reread the Vivid Vision throughout the year. A perfect time to do this is at the start of your quarterly planning retreat. At these retreats, I've found it helpful to have each person read the Vivid Vision quietly and circle the key words or sentences that resonate with them.

Then, go around the room and have each person read aloud what they circled. This exercise provides alignment for the whole team before the brainstorming process takes place, and it is a useful tool to assist you in planning and prioritizing future projects. At MCI, a Geneva-based global association, communications, and event-management partner whose Vivid Vision is shared below, employees actually read one section of the company's Vivid Vision before starting any meeting where three or more people attend. They are maniacal about staying focused on their vision so that all decisions and discussions are aligned with it.

Once you've committed to sketching your vision for the future and painting your picture, you'll be well equipped to reverse engineer your own success.

The Five Core Annual Goals

As discussed, the Vivid Vision is the first and arguably most important step in developing a focus for your business. Ensuring that you as the entrepreneur reread your own Vivid Vision monthly will ensure that you and others around you are focused on making it come true. Ensuring that your employees, customers and suppliers all reread it at least quarterly will really ensure that they are focused on making it a reality as well. It doesn't stop there, however. Vision without execution is hallucination. Pretty sure it was Thomas Edison who first uttered those words. And I live by them. As important as the Vivid

Vision is, we then need to figure out how to make it happen. And it starts by setting some goals to get us there.

Consider that the Vivid Vision will unfold over three years. That means roughly 33 percent of it will come true in the third year, 33 percent in the second year, and 34 percent in the first year. Using this information, you can decide which goals you need to drive toward to finish with a strong first year.

The next step is to identify the five core annual goals you need to hit to help take bring the Vivid Vision to fruition. I coach all entrepreneurs to set a measurable goal for each of these areas. And by measurable I mean that the written goal for each needs to be a dollar sign ($), number sign (#) or percentage symbol (%). Otherwise the goal isn't tight enough. Hazy goals produce hazy results.

I also have a different mindset related to goal setting that makes me more successful than most entrepreneurs. I set the goals then figure out how to make them happen. Most people simply forecast where they will end up. I decide where I want to end up then create the plan that will take me there.

The five goals you need to set include the following:

- Revenue
- Profit
- Customer Engagement
- Employee Engagement
- Strategic Thrust

When you set them, you should consider this information:

Revenue—What do you want your revenue to be three years from now. Work backwards from there. Let's say today your revenue is currently $1 million, and in three years you want your revenue to be $5 million. If you work it backwards, you might see that year two needs to be $3 million, and year one needs to be $2 million.

Profit—Similar to revenue, begin with the end in mind. How much money do you want to make three years from now? Given that number, how much money do you want to make two years out? One year out? That first year profit number is the goal for next year.

You see where we're going here. Thinking three years out and reverse engineering the goals creates the overall picture you're aiming for. Once you have all five goals established, then you can figure out which projects you need to finish to help you hit those goals.

Customer Engagement—This one is easy—only one number matters. It's called Net Promoter Score (NPS). The reality is, most companies don't know how to measure their customer satisfaction, and when they do, they use the wrong number (like an average score out of 10). The number I use is based on the NPS Calculation:

Calculate your NPS using your customers' answers to a single question: On a scale from 0–10, how likely is it that you would recommend [company name] to a friend or colleague? This is called the Net Promoter Score question or the recommend question.

Respondents are grouped as follows:

- *Promoters* (score 9–10) are loyal enthusiasts who will keep buying and refer others, fueling growth.

- *Passives* (score 7–8) are satisfied but unenthusiastic customers who are vulnerable to competitive offerings.

- *Detractors* (score 0–6) are unhappy customers who can damage your brand and impede growth through negative word-of-mouth.

Subtracting the percentage of detractors from the percentage of promoters yields the Net Promoter Score, which can range from a low of -100 (if every customer is a detractor) to a high of 100 (if every customer is a promoter).

My clients all push to get themselves to somewhere between 50–80 percent NPS. It's not easy, but once you know where you are as a benchmark by doing a quick initial survey, then you can establish a goal about where you want to get to this year.

Employee Engagement—This is a critically important and often overlooked goal. The happier your employees are, the happier your customers will be, and the more profitable your company will be. I use the same NPS calculation relied on for customer engagement. However, I ask this question instead:

How likely is it that you would recommend [company name] to a friend or colleague as a place to work?

Strategic Thrust—This goal is often harder to wrap your head around. It's a new strategic push you are making for the company. For example, I'm currently working hard to get the first 50 members signed up for the COO Alliance, the mastermind group I mentioned earlier. So my goal is 50 COO Alliance Members by Dec 31st. Last year it was three new books published on Amazon. Strategically both of those goals moved my brand forward and built new revenue channels. Both are strategic in nature and outside the area of my core focus. Years ago when I helped build 1-800-GOT-JUNK?, one of our annual strategic thrust goals was to have a presence in the top 30 metro areas in the US by 2003. We pushed hard to meet that goal, knowing that, once we were in every major market, it would be hard for a competitor to gain traction. By working hard and focusing, we occupied all 30. In fact, on December 17, 2003, we signed the 30th city, Madison Wisconsin.

A strong clarity around these annual goals is essential for every entrepreneur. Keep in mind, It's not important right now how those goals will be achieved. That will be worked out later. In the beginning, you want to establish the goals and share them with your team and an accountability partner. When I set the goal for each of those five areas for the year, I first think about what the goal for each area will be three years out, two years out, and then one year from now. I work backwards from where I want to be, versus forecasting from where I am.

After you set annual goals, which are based on your Vivid Vision, you plan each goal in the current year and each quarter. You can use your own process and really nail this, but I'll share a rough outline.

Develop a plan identifying no more than 10 key projects that will help fulfill those five annual goals. Plan your work and work your plan. Look for the low-hanging fruit. I seek the easy-to-implement projects that will move the company forward and create momentum.

For example, I spend a lot of time harnessing free PR because it creates the biggest bang for the buck, so to speak. I generate as many media interviews as I can because it drives momentum, revenue, profitability, builds engagement, and costs me no money and very little time.

Too often entrepreneurs focus on projects that will achieve the goals, but are more complex than needed. Instead I highly suggest entrepreneurs look for easy to execute projects that are inexpensive because momentum creates momentum. You can usually get close if not all the way to the goals without more. And the energy created by getting stuff started and finished usually creates more momentum and results than trying to nail some huge, hairy complex project.

I also limit the projects to 10 per year. The reality is you'll likely do more, but by focusing on those 10, you'll get them done, and then you can add to your list later. Staying focused is key. If you start with a project list of 20, you can become overwhelmed, distracted, and will likely get less done overall. Less is more here.

Continue to break the goals and projects into smaller projects and tasks that are completed in the most logical order to get you to completion the fastest. For example, a yearly goal becomes four smaller quarterly goals. Quarterly goals become three smaller monthly goals. Each week, as you look at your strategic projects for the month and the quarter, decide what five things, in order of impact, need to be done to move those forward or bring them to completion. Start with the big items then handle the busy work afterward. Simply committing to the top three to five tasks you'll finish each day, will help you accomplish your large annual and quarterly goals.

How to Roll Out Your Vivid Vision

Internal Rollout

When others read your Vivid Vision, they should experience a moment of awe and wonder. If their jaws don't drop, maybe you are not thinking big enough. Small, safe, calculated plans don't inspire extraordinary action. Imagine the room when Elon Musk announced that he wanted his Model S to go from 0 to 60 miles per hour in 2.8

seconds on something he called ludicrous mode. Someone must have been thinking, "Dude, you're crazy."

Get outside of your comfort zone and into your stretch zone. If you don't have butterflies, no one else will either. It's imperative that others share your enthusiasm. Ultimately, that is why you are crafting your Vivid Vision in the first place. It's not about feeling warm and fuzzy by your own personal vision board that no one else understands. You are going to roll this vision out for the world to see, so be bold when you do.

During the rollout, it is important to let people know that some items within the document will happen sooner than others. Some will not be realized until the end of three years. Those might require things that don't yet exist! You may need to rely on technologies that will be invented, upgraded, or made affordable along the way. It is a stackable vision in that sense, building from foundation to floor to walls, and upward, just like a dream home.

If you don't remind people that getting three years into the future necessitates first accomplishing certain things in year one and two, they will likely overlook that fact and assume you are nuts. It's a bit like telling a 13-year-old what life will be like at 16; they can't even visualize it yet, it seems so far away, and their world will have changed enormously in that span of time.

Share with Everyone in the Company

Begin with the internal rollout. Share your Vivid Vision with your employees, board members, and anyone else inside the walls of the company. It is important to start internally to make sure that everyone on the team really understands it and is excited about before you present it to the outside world.

Everyone within the company must see, feel, and breathe it because these people are points of contact with the outside world. You would not want a supplier getting excited about it and calling an employee who has no idea what the person is talking about. It needs to be completely understood and embraced inside the organization first. Maybe one quarter later, you will execute your external rollout.

Conduct this rollout in-person and alongside your team. Try to get everyone in the same room. This will, of course, depend on the size of your organization. If yours is a 30-person company, you can do it with everyone at once. If you have 500-person company, you probably segment by departments and modify the rollout described below. If yours is a 20,000-person organization, you will have to get creative!

Start with a hard copy of the Vivid Vision. Have the entire group read it aloud with each person reading a portion until the whole document is finished.

While the reading is being done, the CEO's job is to gauge the reaction of the people in the room. Who is engaged, excited, invested? Who isn't? It's that latter group of people that should raise red flags for you. They might not be a good fit for the company—or they might not understand your vision. Make it your mission to find out.

After the group has read through the pages, encourage them to circle the sentences and phrases that most excite them, the ones that inspire them most, and share these with the group.

This is not a forum for discussion or debate. The activity exists to allow employees to understand where the CEO wants to lead the organization. In later meetings, there will be opportunities to discuss how each statement will be accomplished, but for now, the material needs to sink in and provide a source of contemplation and inspiration. You want your people to think, *what if?* and become engaged and aligned with your Vivid Vision.

Bear in mind, the journey is three years long. Each new quarter, you'll want to break out the Vivid Vision again and reread it. Open it as a Word document and highlight in green any of the items that have come to fruition. Then highlight the ones you are currently working on in yellow. Allow everyone to see the future taking shape.

Next, take a look at each sentence and decide which projects need to be tackled next and the actions necessary to accomplish them. This will determine what your quarter is going to look like, and you can chart a course accordingly with these sentences acting as your map.

This exercise will keep everyone in the organization on the same page and in alignment. It will inspire them once again and help them maintain focus. It allows everyone to start figuring out what needs to be done today to fulfill the lofty goals you are pursuing as a group.

After the internal rollout, I suggest waiting about one quarter to begin introducing it to the outside world. The external rollout will provide the document to potential employees, customers, suppliers, potential suppliers, bankers, lawyers, and, of course, the media.

Potential employees will read your Vivid Vision, and they'll either feel excited to interview for a job, or they will know right away that this is not the kind of company they want to work for.

Suppliers will be excited about working with you, and you may even secure better prices than you might have anticipated because they can see where you are taking the company in the future. When your suppliers catch your enthusiasm, cool stuff starts to happen.

I have seen bankers fund an operation based solely on the Vivid Vision because, for the first time, they understand what the company does. Financial statements or a meeting with the CEO don't always provide a clear picture.

I've had potential customers sign contracts because they were so excited by what the future of the company looked like. They bet on the future of the company instead of its current state.

You gain leverage by sharing your plan with the media. You want them telling the story of your future, rather than what it looks like today. When the media starts talking about what the company will look like in three years, people pay attention.

Everyone wants to peek into the future and for good reason. Whatever interaction a customer has with a company will probably involve a relationship that lasts for a year or more. Even if it is as simple as a manufacturer's warranty, the customer wants to know that, in a year's time, the company will still be around.

Here's a concrete example. Let's say you were going to rent a condo, and when you walked into the model unit, the floors were dirty, walls needed painting, and the lighting was crummy. You would not want to rent the place. But what if the owner said, "By the way, I'm putting in new floors tomorrow, painting next week, and replacing all the lights. Let me show you the place next door that was refurbished last week"? You would feel differently because you've had a glimpse of the future. And that is the purpose of sharing the Vivid Vision with the outside world. Others will be able to see what you can see.

If you have been bold enough in your ideas, your Vivid Vision will produce two effects: It will attract some people and repel others. Notice I said it will attract *and* repel, not *or* repel. Your Vivid Vision should behave like a magnet, drawing some people in and pushing others—hopefully not too many—away. If your scope is too small, too milquetoast, too watered down, if everyone likes it, then no one will love it. If this is the case, you have failed.

Be Revolutionary, Not Evolutionary

Remember when Apple launched the iPhone? People thought the company had gone crazy because it didn't have a keyboard. *How can you release a smart phone that doesn't have a keyboard? That is absurd.*

Some people loved it though. Not only did they love it, they loved it a lot, and branded themselves loyal and devoted Apple customers. They stood in long lines for product launches with other like-minded consumers.

Meanwhile, those who hated the iPhone could only watch the effect the device had on the rest of the industry. Other companies attempted to copy the design and compete in a market that Apple had conquered. These companies realized that keyboards would soon be as obsolete as VCRs, and eventually they were forced to convert, willingly or kicking and screaming.

Had Apple tried to make everybody happy when it designed the revolutionary phone, they would simply have made a more polished version of the existing Blackberry. Strive for a bold vision like this if you want to inspire people. And take for granted that a backlash will happen. After all, the future is scary to people who have become too comfortable in the present.

The 15 Percent

I once worked with a client on the internal rollout for his company. The CEO stood up and said, "About 15 percent of you are going to hate what you hear. You're not going to like what the future holds in store for you, but that's OK. It's probably the right time for you to quit."

Sure enough, about 15 percent of his employees did quit. Two years later, his company was ranked as the second best company to work for in British Columbia (incidentally, the number one company to work for was another client of mine who had also inspired everyone with a bold Vivid Vision).

It is fine to lose people who don't get it. You don't want those people around in the first place. It's better to know on day one that they are not aligned than try to encourage them for two years with great frustration.

The same is true of potential employees. Your potential employees will read your document and either think *Hell yeah, I want to interview here*, or *Hell no, I don't want to go anywhere near that place*. Now, you're not wasting time interviewing those people, much less money on hiring and training them. At the end of the day, when everyone can see where you are going, you save time and money.

One last point on this matter. The Vivid Vision is like the Ten Commandments in that it is set in stone. The only time it should be changed is if there is a massive and unexpected industry transformation or if your company executes a 90-degree pivot. If there is a global financial crisis and your world just got turned upside down or if your building collapses.

Otherwise, you are a ship going across the ocean, tacking left and right, dodging icebergs when necessary, but always going in the same general direction. Don't worry if a few sentences become moot along the way. Just let them be. This document is a beacon of light safely guiding your crew.

External Rollout

Recipients

The external rollout lets everybody understand where the organization is heading, why that's exciting, and why their perspective of your company should be based on the point three years from now rather than today.

Just as with the internal rollout among your team, it is critical to ease the minds of people who might think the idea sounds crazy. Reassure them that some concepts are still a year or two away and that, once the initial items are in place, the final components won't seem so farfetched.

Introduce your Vivid Vision by saying, "This is what our company is going to look like in the near future. We all recognize it doesn't look like this today, but this is us leaning out three years in the future and describing what it looks, acts, and feels like." This rollout should go out simultaneously.

Once everyone within the organization fully understands the Vivid Vision and is rallying behind it, you can share it with the rest of the world. Use email blasts, a post on the company website, newsletters, press conferences, journalist pitches, flyers, bullhorns, stopping people on the street—OK, there might be a limit to how far you go to get the message out, but definitely err on the side of spreading the word.

Continually sending it to people is key. You want everyone who is relevant to your company in some way to see what you are building, where you are going, and what it looks like. These outside parties play a role in your vision as they contribute and conspire to make it come true.

There is no point in making plans for the future if you don't know what the future holds. And because you want others to include you in their future plans, it is imperative that you remind them of what your future looks like. If you are orienting yourself in the wilderness, it is crucial to keep looking at the map to know where you are and the way you intend to go. The same is true of the Vivid Vision: It is a map of the future that you and others can follow.

Possible Reasons for Doubt or Fear

One people fear in the external rollout is their competitors. Given the extremely personal nature of the Vivid Vision, there is a tendency to worry that someone will try to steal your ideas. And while that feeling is real, in actuality, no one else has the ability to execute *your* ideas.

Remember, you are only showing them the final product, they have no idea how to get there. You won't show anyone your business plan, just your destination. And once you announce where you are going, you have staked out that territory. Should anyone else attempt to plant their flag there, it will come off as derivative, as if that company does not have enough vision to chart its own course.

The other reason people get nervous about the unveiling process is that they don't yet know a crucial element involved in it: *the how*. Vulnerability is a natural result of not having all the answers. It is difficult to stand in front of a room of people and make a bold announcement when you worry that someone will ask, "How are you going to make that happen?" and you don't have a plan yet.

Again, remember, that it is not your job to have that answer. Omniscience is not a prerequisite for being the head of a company. *You have people for that.* The way that you answer the question is that your team, in whom you have the utmost trust, will simply get it done because that is the task you have given them.

Reasons for Sharing with the World

What ends up happening as a result your focused campaign to share your vision with the world is that the world comes to accept it. Sometimes it happens suddenly, and people wake up and see what you have told them to see. The blinders have come off, and the world as you have described it, appears before them. Now, you have converted others to your way of thinking, like the way Henry Fonda's character wins over the other 11 men on the jury in *12 Angry Men*.

That change in perspective can trigger a chain reaction within your organization and without. Inside, everybody begins to see and feel what you do. They are able to make decisions much more intuitively, understanding that they, too, have seen the Vivid Vision in reality.

Outside, people look in and see that your organization functions as a single unit, and they begin to realize that in three years' time, you really will have achieved that big, hairy, audacious goal. To that end, walk certain core customers through the future of your company so they don't hear about it from a random source. Walk your suppliers through it, so they know where you are going. Consider who would benefit from seeing the bigger picture.

When we were building 1-800-Got-Junk?, we sat down with the supplier who made the blue boxes for the back of the trucks, and we showed them what our company would look like three years out. He said, "I'm glad you told me. We do not have anywhere near that number of trucks even ordered for North America next year."

We needed him to be aware of our needs to fulfill our vision of the future. As a result, the supplier planned for our future expansion. Since it required his needs to change, he could make those plans to support the company. Before you know it, everyone in the chain was scaling up based on our expectations.

People not only want to work for cutting edge companies, they want to work with them as well. If you are a customer talking about doubling your growth in three years, others will pay attention because they want to grow alongside you. As a result, you will get more of their time and service and maybe even a better rate. Again, you want to be treated as the company you will become, not the one you currently are, so share your Vivid Vision with your suppliers.

A Dancing Guy, Jet Pilots, and Bricklayers

Often, getting others to see your organization as you see it is simply a matter of perseverance. An example of that is evident in a video from the Sasquatch Music Festival from several years back. This video went viral, and I enjoy sharing it as an illustration of the power of one person's ideas. One guy at the festival dances by himself. Not in a sad way because he seems happy enough, but he dances alone.

A big crowd has gathered on the grassy hillside. Still alone, the guy continues to dance. After a while, one other guy joins him. The two guys dance. Then, a third guy walks up and starts to dance.

Moments later, people run down the hillside to participate in this little group of dancing guys. Thousands upon thousands of people are dancing in the same fashion as that one guy who only minutes before, was dancing all by himself. A tipping point occurred, and suddenly, everyone's thinking has changed.

You are going to have to win others to your side. And along the way, you will be challenged and may be ridiculed. People within your own building may begin to doubt the viability of the Vivid Vision.

This, of course, is why it is so important to keep reading the document aloud and to keep sharing it with others outside the organization. But even so, you will encounter obstacles along the way. The best way to overcome those obstacles is to align as tightly as possible and move forward as a single unit.

Think about jet pilots, like the team of Blue Angels. At ridiculous speeds in a sky that has no demarcations or signage, the pilots weave in and out of various formations with deftness, beauty, and grace. How do they do it? They are perfectly aligned.

If these pilots did not follow their maneuvers to the letter, a collision would be inevitable. Each pilot must know not only what his job is, but also he must know what the other guys are doing. Just as important, if not more so, he has to trust that they will do their jobs and do them perfectly. This is how you want your operation to run—smoothly and almost by instinct.

The beauty of this kind of alignment is certainly on full display as you and your team pursue that lofty three-year goal, but there are other times when this sort of intuitive functioning is needed for the company to make a 90-degree pivot. Getting people on the same page in a pivot can be as unwieldy as trying to back a semi down a one-way alley. Or it can be as smooth as a couple of jets zigzagging across an empty sky: the difference is alignment.

It is becoming more and more difficult to establish and maintain alignment in the modern workplace. A major reason for this is off-site work. Remote employees can be difficult to keep aligned. The same is true of freelancers, independent contractors, part-time and temporary workers, and other truthfully essential members of your workforce who are employees on site full time. And yet, in 2016, these are often crucial players in a successful business venture.

It is important, therefore, that these people really understand what the big picture is and how they fit into it. There's an analogy that works here of a man walking down the street who meets three other men making bricks. He asks the first guy, "What are you doing?"

The first of the trio says, "I'm making bricks."

The man asks the second brickmaker, "What are you doing?"

And the second guy says, "I'm making these bricks to build a wall."

The man asks the third brickmaker, "What are you doing?"

And the third guy says, "I'm making these bricks to build the wall of a glorious cathedral that will be used for the worship of God."

Who do you think feels a greater alignment of purpose every morning when he goes to work? They all perform the same function, but the third one understands why they are making bricks, and he understands the significance of those bricks.

If you'd like help to make your Vivid Vision jump off the page, email me at VividVision@CameronHerold.com, and we can introduce you to one of the writers who produces the final versions for all of our clients.

Entrepreneur Profile

W. Brett Wilson, Dragon Emeritus
(and whatnot)

W. Brett Wilson's company is Prairie Merchant Corporation.

Top Business Accomplishments

❖ Brett co-founded FirstEnergy Capital Corp. in 1993, where he was president and chairman. The company started with $2 million of capital and was valued at $300 million 15 years later when 20 percent was sold to Société Général.

❖ He faced work addiction during his iBanking career, but turned it around to build great relationships with his children.

❖ He has become a leader in Canada and elsewhere in the use of strategic philanthropy to grow a business. He has received awards for his efforts in this area, including the Order of Canada and the Saskatchewan Order of Merit.

❖ He landed a celebrated role in the Gemini-Award winning episodes of *Dragons' Den*, a show that attracted record audiences in Canada during his seasons and changed the way that Canadian's perceive and celebrate entrepreneurship.

❖ He has invested successfully in a wide range of assets, from office buildings to a high-performing NHL Hockey Team to extensive holdings of farmland in Saskatchewan. He is the co-lead investor in an independent power producer (Maxim Power) and early stage investor in scores of successful Canadian oil and gas producers. Currently, he is the Chairman of Canoe Financial, Canada's fastest growing mutual fund company.

Morning Routine

❖ Brett starts his day by drinking a glass of water with lemon juice.

❖ He checks the overnight news, his social media accounts, and email.

❖ He works out for 15 minutes while watching news feeds.

❖ Then he spends time chilling with his dog and Bullet Proof coffee.

❖ He usually works from home for an hour or more in the morning, which allows him quiet time to focus on laying out his day.

— 8 —

ENTREPRENEUR ELEVATION PRINCIPLE #2:

DELEGATE EVERYTHING EXCEPT GENIUS

As all entrepreneurs know, you live and die by your ability to prioritize. You must focus on the most important, mission-critical tasks each day and night, and then share, delegate, delay or skip the rest.
—JESSICA JACKLEY, Co-founder of Kiva

The role of the entrepreneur, extensive as it might be, is not to do everything. If you are doing everything, you're being terribly inefficient with your time and resources. The best way to get things done is by delegating everything except genius. In other words, if there are others who can do the job, let them. And if there aren't, you might not be thinking hard enough to find someone—

because there usually is. Entrepreneur Dave Feller, who is the CEO of Mogo Financial, prides himself on being "the lazy entrepreneur." When I first met Dave, he told me that he started his company in a city that was 2,000 miles away from where he lived so that he wouldn't and couldn't get sucked into the day-to-day running of the business. He knew that, by having the office so far away, he would be forced to hire people and delegate more than if he was around the employees. Even the distractions stopped because no one could pop in to see "if he had a minute to talk" about projects they were working on.

Think about the chores involved in running a household. If you're a busy professional, you have enough projects to worry about, but if you're also tasked with scrubbing the toilet, mopping the floors, and washing the windows, you're frittering away valuable time doing work that can be farmed out to literally anyone. And because it *can* be, it *should* be. Hire someone else to do the mundane jobs and use your time to accomplish the things that no one else can do. At the end of the day, it is likely you are great at a few areas of your business. The more time you focus on those core areas, the more money you'll make. Think about your personal life this way and start making a list of all the things you can hire someone, likely at $12–15 per hour, to do for you.

Potential Personal Areas You Can Outsource

- House cleaning
- Laundry
- Ironing
- Dropping off & Picking Up Dry Cleaning
- Household Chores
- Minor house repairs
- Yard cleaning
- Cleaning up after parties
- Lawn cutting
- Deliveries
- Grocery shopping

- Food prep & cooking meals for the week
- Taking things to post office or courier
- Taking kids to school or picking them up from school or activities

As you can see, this list is virtually endless…

Begin by creating an activity inventory of everything you do in your role as an entrepreneur. This is a list you should draw up every six to twelve months, compiling everything that you do in your day-to-day job as an entrepreneur. Imagine if someone followed you around constantly with a video camera to record all the things they saw you do, big and small, during your waking hours in running your business. For me, this includes reading email, setting up meetings, attending meetings, talking to authors and writers, setting up flights, hotel bookings, car services, preparing for coaching calls, designing worksheets, reviewing sites and speakers for the COO Alliance, among dozens of other tasks. It's actually pretty endless. You need to start thinking about it this way: tasks need to be done, but that doesn't mean that you need to be the one doing it all.

Now, chart those actions in an Excel spreadsheet. Use one row per task and write down as many tasks as you can honestly see yourself having done or doing during a normal month or quarter. You'll take your entire activity inventory and figure out how to handle it all without being as involved as you are today

Your all-inclusive list might include 60, 70, or even 80 things for that period. And after you have done a full mind dump of all these activities, you'll begin to categorize them to help you get them off your plate. You can also keep adding to this list as you go, but try to get as many listed before you work with it. The next step is to categorize the activities in a second column in one of four ways. Mark one of these four letters in the column beside where you've listed the tasks:

- *I* stands for Incompetent: You suck at them.
- *C* stands for Competent: You're "okay" at them.

- *E* stands for Excellent: You're excellent at them, but you don't love doing them.

- *U* stands for Unique Ability: These tasks energize you, and you're also really good at them.

The test I use to determine if something is a unique ability is whether I would do it for free if my kids didn't have to eat. If the answer is yes, that's a *U* in the second column of the spreadsheet. My unique ability, for example, is speaking to and coaching CEOs. Anytime I'm doing anything other than a speaking event or a coaching session, I'm typically working on stuff that I might be good at, but that I don't necessarily get energized by. If you can start delegating everything that you're not awesome at and that doesn't give you energy, then you're well on your way to rapid entrepreneurial success. If you're really careful about calling things unique ability, you will likely only have two to three things on your plate that are Us. The rest are more correctly categorized as *E* or *C*.

The third column involves assigning a dollar figure. If you were paying someone to do this one task, what would you pay as an hourly rate. Would you pay $10 an hour, which is a $20,000 a year job? Would you pay $20 an hour, which is $40,000 a year job? Some of the tasks on your list are literally so beneath you from a dollar perspective that it makes no sense whatsoever for you to be doing them. You'd be far better off paying someone $15–20 an hour to do these tasks while you get paid 10–100 times that for working in your unique ability. My time is so highly leveraged when I'm doing speaking events or coaching CEOs, that doing anything but those activities or finding more opportunities to do them constitutes my being inefficient with my time. Think of it this way. You only have three resources: people, time and money. Your job is to get the highest return on each of those and not waste any.

Now you have a column that lists all your activities (one per row), a second column that lists your competency in each activity, and a third column that shows a dollar amount that you would be willing to pay for someone to take that activity off your plate. You should delegate everything in the incompetency, competency, and excellent categories that falls beneath your pay rate as an entrepreneur.

Pay someone to do those tasks, otherwise, you are essentially hiring a CEO to do them at your personal hourly rate. In fact, as soon as possible, get everything off your plate that you rated incompetent or competent. Then work to delegate the excellent tasks too. Also consider whether you need to keep doing these tasks at all. Perhaps they're better off being on your stop doing list than your to-do List going forward.

The next thing to do is something I learned from Suzanne Evans, one of the entrepreneurs I coach. She'll sit down first thing in the morning and make an all-inclusive list of all the stuff that needs to get done during the day, and then she tries to delegate 80 percent of it. She will work on only 20 percent of whatever is on her list for the day. Strive to reach that number by delegating responsibilities. Imagine if right after you wrote your weekly or daily to-do list that you also decided who you could outsource or delegate 80 percent of the tasks to instead of your going head down and diving into them yourself.

The 80 percent figure is not a coincidence. We've all heard of the Pareto principle, where 80 percent of your results come from 20 percent of your efforts. Knowing this is true, why not focus only on your unique ability areas? That simple idea alone will help you get much higher results. The 80 percent figure is also a mindset that will help you when perfection isn't necessary. We often get bogged down in perfectionism, which can lead to procrastination. If you spend your precious time trying to write the perfect memo, design the perfect ad, or achieve some kind of transcendence on a task outside the realm of your unique ability, you should stop aiming so high. Get it to 80 percent and find a specialist who is capable of perfecting it from there. Most people are quite fine with an 80 percent result. Most people don't need perfect at all. So as an entrepreneur, keep focused on delegating everything except genius as much as you can.

Remember your job is to see the big picture. Don't get bogged down in the details. Use your resources wisely. Get items off your plate as quickly as possible so that you can focus your attention elsewhere.

Look for other areas of your life where you are paying a CEO's salary for work that could be accomplished by a high school kid: running clothes to the dry cleaner, going to the grocery store, cooking meals, cleaning house, and so on. Use the time that you save to work within your unique ability or to savor the moments of your life and recharge your batteries.

There are plenty of apps and websites that can help you delegate tasks. Sites such as Upwork, oDesk, Fiverr, and HireMyMom.com, for instance, provide relief for the busy entrepreneur. Each of these websites have free tutorials or use YouTube to learn how best to use them. You can list tons of individual projects that need to get done, and people from around the world will bid on how little they will charge you to do that work.

You can use project management apps, such as Basecamp and Asana, that give you the tools to identify and manage daily tasks and long-term projects. Both of those websites have some fantastic videos to show you how using them can leverage your time.

You can even look into using companies like Less Doists run by Ari Meisel that have a staff of executive assistants whom you literally meet with on a weekly basis to discuss everything on your plate. They, in turn, handle that stuff for you. They will handle the project management and hiring of people, so that you don't have to worry about that. They'll literally help pull stuff off your plate.

Entrepreneurs are often their own worst enemies. Because we often start a business with no employees, we can, and often have done, almost every job in some way, shape, or form. So we're used to diving in headfirst and getting stuff done. Remember though, as an entrepreneur, you need to get stuff done, but you don't need to be the person to do it all.

It has been only in the last decade and a half that the new online freelance economy developed. You couldn't find these people in the Yellow Pages or in classified ads in the back of the newspaper. Back then, you had to hire full-time employees, who were jacks of all trades and masters of none. But now, you can find experts and specialists in your own backyard and around the world who are willing to perform tasks. They're looking to do pretty much everything that's on your list, and they're talented. For every task, someone does it well and loves doing it. My cleaning lady is a great example. She loves to do housework. And she's really great at it—my closet is organized as nicely as any of the best clothing stores.

As I said before, one of the most important things that I learned early on as an entrepreneur is that if you don't have an assistant, you are one. A lot of people wait to hire their second in command, but the reality is, what they need to do first is hire somebody to take a lot of the busywork off their plates. Executive assistants are pretty much the biggest leverage you can give yourself in the early days of building your company. My executive assistant, Meridith Kuba, is fantastic. She loves helping me, and I can't imagine running my business today or in the future without her. She has the ability to do things faster and better than me. And she's always happy to take more off my plate.

At some point, after you've hired an executive assistant, you're going to start looking to build your team, hire employees, and find a second in command. That's a really big step, but an effective one. Usually more expensive than the other staff you'll hire, but when you can start delegating and getting big projects off your plate—projects that you might be excellent at but which don't energize you—that's where a good COO comes into play. This is the person who will be able to take those projects off your plate.

At the end of the day, you have only three resources: people, time, and money. Spend each one of those to get the greatest return on your investment. As far as your time is concerned, it should be spent either to maximize its financial return or to maximize your happiness and provide you a better life. And the best way to achieve either of those results is to delegate everything except your genius.

Entrepreneur Profile

Marie Forleo

Marie Forleo's company is Marie Forleo International

Top Business Accomplishments

❖ Marie was named by Oprah as a Thought Leader for the Next Generation.

❖ Her company was named an *Inc. 500 Fastest Growing Company* of 2014.

❖ She writes, produces, and hosts MarieTV, one of the most influential online shows for creatives and entrepreneurs, which has over 22 million views and an audience in 195 countries.

❖ MarieForleo.com was named among the Top 100 Websites for Entrepreneurs by Forbes.com.

❖ Marie firmly believes that every sale changes lives. Because with every product sold, her company supports a person in need.

Morning Routine

❖ For Marie, no two days are ever the same.

❖ She wakes up at different times based on travel, where she's living and working, her shooting schedules, etc. So, what actually happens in the morning shifts for her quite often. Some habits are nonnegotiable because they keep her productive and sane.

❖ She does at least 10 minutes of meditation.

❖ She drinks coffee or green juice.

❖ She must exercise. That varies from spin to yoga to dance to classes. It also doesn't have to happen in the morning for her. Sometimes it makes more sense for it to happen at night.

❖ One other *evening* habit that she considers to be a game changer for entrepreneurs is planning her days out the night before. That makes the morning *way* more productive, enjoyable, and stress free.

Entrepreneur Elevation Principle #3:

YIN YANG:
A COO to LEVERAGE YOU

Do not hire a man who does your work for money, but him who does it for the love of it.
—HENRY DAVID THOREAU

I launched the COO Alliance (www.COOAlliance.com) because I recognized the important, impactful role this position plays for the CEO. Entrepreneurs reap great value from a group dedicated to the people who occupy this critical second-in-command office. The COO, when you hire one, will produce a massively powerful and positive impact on your business. COO means chief operating officer, though often it would be the same as a general manager or a vice president for operations, but with a more senior title.

Entrepreneurs build companies, but at some point, they need someone who can run the day-to-day operations for them. It makes sense that sharing the load would lighten the CEO's burden. He can then afford to take a sick day or get a good night's sleep. It also allows them to focus their energies on the two or three things at which they excel and are uniquely capable of doing. Entrepreneurs are visionaries, but they often lack the detail orientation to get things done and in the right way.

This relationship provides a yin and yang dynamic. It is a unique form of balance at the very core of the company, a business soul mate for the CEO. When I worked as a COO at 1-800-GOT-JUNK?, I established a weekly meeting with the CEO to keep us in sync. It was akin to a date night not only to keep your finger on the pulse of matters, but also to build the relationship, communication, and trust between you and your COO. And as an Entrepreneur or CEO, you need to understand that these meetings are necessary for your second in command if you want that person on the same page as you. You should keep these meetings no matter what; they are critical. More than any other business relationship as you grow, the CEO-COO relationship is key to your growth because this key person will often take larger operational and strategic projects off your plate. They'll often end up with entire areas of the company reporting to them so that you can better leverage your time.

I've talked about this topic at the COO Alliance and heard a variety of ways that these face time meetings occur. One that I find especially compelling is the idea of a morning run. Getting fresh air, watching the sun come up, and getting your body moving is a great way to avoid the distractions of cell phones, email, and shop talk. It's a very human connection that allows for great conversation and rapport building. Chip Wilson, the founder and former CEO of Lululemon, loved to take hikes with his COO. Steve Jobs was famous for his "walk and talks" too.

When I was COO at 1-800-GOT-JUNK?, the CEO, Brian, and I decided to train for a half marathon together. I ran two of them two years in a row, and we had six months where we ran on Tuesday and Thursday mornings at 6:30 a.m., and it was amazing. Running with someone for 45 to 90 minutes and talking through the facts, feelings, restrainers, or drivers facing each of you. Even if you're not talking work, you're still having a human connection with the most important person in your business world.

It's important for these two people at the heart of a company to understand each other beyond a casual and professional level. Your COO should know intuitively which problems to bring to you and which to resolve without the need of consultation. As CEO, you have a lot to deal with, so the more your second-in-command can do to keep obstructions out of your way, the more you can focus on the bigger issues. Your COO has to read your mind *and* anticipate things you may not.

That level of trust does not happen without conscious effort, as I've heard again and again at the COO Alliance. Most CEOs don't want to deal with every minute detail of a problem; they want a summary and a resolution. But that requires a communication plan to filter questions and know what needs to be seen and when, what constitutes success, what sorts of empowerment and support are available, conflict-management strategies, and established operating principles that dictate the boundaries of the COO's decision making.

Before you hire a COO, you need to be honest with yourself about what your weaknesses are and identify the areas of the job you don't love doing so you can find someone who has strengths in those areas and enjoys those aspects of the business. I read a helpful article in the *Harvard Business Review* called "The Misunderstood Role of the COO" that addresses precisely this. They discovered seven different types of COOs: outward facing, inward facing, technology focused, sales and marketing focused, operational focused, engineering and product focused, and financial focused. Seven completely different types of COOs, so when you say, "I need a second in command," it's kind of like saying, "How high is up?" You need to be clear about the important skills that are not within the scope of your unique abilities. Then find the COO whose unique abilities match with what you need.

For example, if you really hate IT and finance, like I do, then you shouldn't be doing them. If you were hiring a second in command for my company, you would be looking for someone who loved those two functions. That would, if nothing else, allow you to push those items off your plate to someone who relishes them.

Suppose that you're not a very detail-oriented person. Then you want someone who can get down in the weeds and monitor the metrics while you take more of a bird's-eye view of matters. Or maybe you have a strong vision of where the company should go, but you are terrible at starting projects. In that case, find a COO with a great deal of initiative, who can get the ball rolling while you concentrate on growing the business.

That said, more often than not the people I talk to who think about hiring a second in command don't even have an executive assistant yet. First things first: hire your executive assistant. After that, you should have about six months before you need a second in command. Be careful when you do that you don't give the person a title that is beyond them. Unless that person really is a COO, you end up paying a lot more than you should, the person gets an inflated sense of importance, or they're trying to fill a role that requires much more seniority.

Consider starting with a title of general manager, which could lead to a director or vice president of operations title. The COO title is appropriate when your company gets to about 100 employees.

When you are ready to hire your second in command, build a scorecard that you can look back on in a year's time to evaluate their work. On that scorecard, list the five big things that your COO would have needed to accomplish to validate the hiring. In the interview process, look for people who have already done as many of those five things as possible and are proficient at doing them.

When you're hiring a COO think about the four categories that you looked at in the last chapter: incompetent, competent, excellent (but don't love doing), and unique abilities you love doing. My unique ability is speaking events and coaching entrepreneurs. Outside of that, I have lots of stuff I'm good at, but I freaking love this.

If you find a COO or second in command who fills one of the seven areas you want them to really focus on, and they can take on the tasks and projects that you're excellent at but don't love, so that you deal only with the stuff that you would do for free, that's step one. That doesn't mean you win, though.

What a lot of people don't realize is that Brian and I didn't get lucky with 1-800-GOT-JUNK?, when we built it. I had already established two franchisors before joining Brian. We didn't get lucky because we had been in a forum in the Entrepreneurs Organization together for three years prior to my joining him as his COO. I had run a private currency company that had just sold for $60 million. I had been working on an auto body chain, and he watched my progress, so he intuitively knew me as a leader, and had interviewed me for three years. He knew my skill set, and that it matched his deficits. He also knew that where he was strong, I was weak. That was step two, was that actually really knew that I could do what he needed me to do.

The next area is trust. A month and a half before I joined Brian as his second-in-command, he was the best man at my first wedding. We were best friends. I've been with him through challenging personal events, including his divorce, that you don't normally hear about or know, except in a strong personal friendship. Our relationship as CEO and COO was like an unbelievable marriage. People wrote stories about us because of that. When you're hiring a second-in-command, you have to interview and hire for that level of implicit trust.

You have to have a good idea of what you're looking for first. In *Alice in Wonderland,* the Cheshire Cat said, "If you don't know where you're going, any road will take you there." So, step one in knowing what you're hiring for is to look at the five big things this person must get done over the next twelve months. Not what they are going to do, but what do they *need to achieve?* Take that information to recruit and interview people who have *done it before.* As I mentioned, I had already built College Pro Painters and Gerber Auto Collision as well as coached franchisors. Coming into 1-800-GOT-JUNK? was cakewalk because I'd had the experience, that is, until we hit about 3,000 employees, and then it got big.

Again, hire people who have done what you need them to do. The scorecard is the measurable part of your job description. The less concrete part is finding your business soul mate, someone you can absolutely trust.

On day one, when a new COO comes in, you give them access to your phone numbers, bank account numbers, and passwords. If you're not willing to give any of that to the person, don't hire them.

To be clear, you are looking for people with experience doing these tasks, rather than people who are merely qualified to do them. If you hire people based on what they might be capable of, you tend to get people who know *how* to do stuff, but if you hire people based on their experience, you get people who have demonstrated that they are capable of *doing* that what you need.

Bear in mind that the best candidates are not looking for a job because they already have jobs. In fact, they're happy and have no intention of leaving for an inferior position. Therefore, you'll need to engage an executive search firm to help you find the right person. And if you're going to spend $200,000 to $400,000 on your COO, it behooves you to go with a search firm that has done this kind of hire before. In other words, you're not posting an ad on Craigslist. You have to seek out someone of that caliber and typically don't have a big enough network to do it on your own.

The best athletes move from one team to another. How many come up from the Farm League or the juniors and join the majors? Not very many, right? One percent, two percent, five percent? Most of them move from one team to another or are traded. Your A player, the specific COO that you're looking for and that can meet your needs, is not on Monster and Craigslist looking for a job. In fact, for any role in your company, the best players won't be looking. You need to be looking for them, and when you find them, strategically woo them.

Your job descriptions have to be written to attract someone who perfectly fits with you. Your job description has to be written in the way that when your ideal candidate reads it, he's like, "Heck yeah, I am all in." So, if you swear, I want you to swear in your job description. I want you to say, "I'm a CEO who's slightly manic, who's doing this, and who swears a bit too much, and blah, blah, blah." Because you know what? If somebody comes in and goes, "I don't like that you swear," your response can be, "Cool, see ya. I don't love that I swear either, but if you're going to work with me, we have to at least gel at the starting point, right?" The first draft of your job description should be like you're telling your best friend. Then, hand it to a marketing person or copywriter, a really good one. You can expect to pay a thousand bucks to have a copywriter make that job description pop off the page. It will read like the best sales copy you've ever read in your life.

Why would we ever write our marketing copy and our landing pages using a copywriter and then use a job description that human resources wrote? They are not experts at crafting descriptions targeted at a particular person. Remember, your ideal COO should read it and say, "Absolutely, yes! I want that role."

Finally, as you make your decision on your COO, you want to bring in someone who is going to make a splash, or more precisely, cause a ripple effect within your organization and beyond. Think of these candidates as boulders, and the job is to get to the bottom of a pond. What kind of stir will this person create? Your job as the CEO is to look for the ripple effect. If that boulder sinks to the bottom without making any waves, your pond is going to be stagnant. Then again, you don't want to cause a tsunami, either.

The perfect COO in your organization starts with, and is about, the relationship you develop. And, you must develop a strong relationship with your COO. (In case I haven't made that clear!) Get to know their desires, dreams, passions, fears, insecurities, and what they hate at work. The bond you form will mean that they will go through brick walls for you, and you will go through brick walls for them, which means it will take the time it takes to develop (and is worth every moment and effort). Build that time into your calendar for that weekly meeting date after they're hired. I used to call it date night for the CEO and COO, but you can go for breakfast once a week in the mornings and have your one-on-one meeting there.

Brian and I actually had a special room at the company that no one even knew about, an old storage room back by a freight elevator. We had two crash pads, a couple of chairs, and a white board. We would duck into the room when no one was watching and we'd sit for an hour. It was our private war room. We had such a tight bond, but we also had our tight space so we could be in that space together.

You've hired your ideal COO, scheduled regular dates, and found your war room. What's next? Don't get too involved in their business. You need to let them do their job. Let them fail or succeed and run it their way. As long as they're aligned with your Vivid Vision, and building it within your core values, you need to let them have some rope. If you tighten up too much, they're going to be restricted, and everybody's going to see and feel it.

I know what you're thinking. *How do I know if it's being done right? How do I check in on the team?* You use a skip level meeting. All of your direct team rolls up, and you can actually see what's happening in their area. But, you need a skip level meeting opportunity to meet with the COO's direct reports. Let's say you want to meet with sales and marketing team, even though that team reports to the CEO or COO.

This is a delicate operation. I can talk to the sales and marketing team when the vice president of sales is absent, but only about where we're going or for feedback. But I can't engage. If the team says there's a problem with an area, I have to listen, and I can ask questions and take notes, but I can't tell you, "Oh, I wish that changed." I can't engage. You need to be careful not to overstep the boundaries and into a role that's really not yours, which could damage the relationship you've worked so hard to build.

Your COO will make a huge difference in your ability to focus on the projects that use your unique abilities and that you love—in other words, they will free you up to do the most valuable work you can do to grow your company. Do the legwork to find the ideal person for the role, work on that relationship as you would your marriage, stay out of the way, and you will forge an unstoppable team to bring your Vivid Vision to fruition over and over again.

Now, set yourself up for entrepreneurial success by taking the Miracle Morning 30-Day Life Transformation Challenge.

Entrepreneur Profile

James Altucher

James Altucher's company is Choose Yourself Media

Top Business Accomplishments

❖ James built and sold Reset, Inc., one of the first designers and software developers for corporate websites in the 1990s, for $15 million. The company created the original websites for AmericanExpress.com, TimeWarner.com, Sony, BMG, Miramax, Loud Records, Bad Boy Records, Con Edison, HBO, and many more.

❖ He wrote *Choose Yourself!* in 2013. With over 600,000 copies sold, it was a *Wall Street Journal* bestseller several times. His book has repeatedly been #1 on Amazon for all nonfiction. He's written 17 other books as well.

❖ *The James Altucher Show* episodes have been downloaded over 20,000,000 times since the show first came out in January 2014.

❖ He managed to switch careers and completely reinvent himself from scratch many times. He has been a software developer, made a TV show, and started many companies. He has been a speaker, writer, hedge fund manager, successful angel investor, and entrepreneur.

❖ He started Choose Yourself Media in 2015. This business was built around monetizing some of his content. The first year revenues were $16 million with a net income of $1.5 million.

Morning Routine

❖ James wakes at 5:30 a.m.

❖ He drinks coffee and reads for the first two hours.

❖ He writes during the second two hours of his day. Usually in these two hours, he will record ten ideas (to keep exercising his "idea muscle") and write an article or a chapter in a book.

❖ Then he eats. This might be his main meal of the day. He goes back and forth about whether fruit is good in the morning or if some form of protein is better, but in general, he avoids processed sugars.

❖ He exercises or walks, takes a nap, makes calls for business and to friends. If he hasn't written an article, then he makes no calls but gets back to reading and writing.

❖ Then he reads and writes some more, which takes him into the evening.

— 10 —

THE MIRACLE MORNING 30-DAY TRANSFORMATION CHALLENGE

An extraordinary life is all about daily, continuous improvements in the areas that matter most.
—ROBIN SHARMA

Let's play devil's advocate for a moment. Can the Miracle Morning really transform any area of your life or business in just 30 days? Can anything really make *that* significant an impact that quickly? Well, remember that it has already done this for thousands of others, and if it works for them, it can and will absolutely work for you.

Incorporating or changing any habit requires an acclimation period, so don't expect this to be effortless from day one. However, by making a commitment to yourself to stick with this, beginning each day with a Miracle Morning and leveraging the Life S.A.V.E.R.S. will quickly become the foundational habit that makes all others possible. Remember: *Win the morning, and you set yourself up to win the day.*

The seemingly unbearable first few days to change a habit are only temporary. While plenty will debate how long it takes to implement a new habit, there is a powerful three-phase strategy that has proven successful for the tens of thousands of individuals who have learned to conquer the snooze button and who now wake up every day for their Miracle Morning.

From Unbearable to Unstoppable:
The Three-Phase Strategy to Implement Any Habit in 30 Days

As you take the Miracle Morning 30-Day Life Transformation Challenge, here's arguably the simplest and most effective strategy for implementing and sustaining any new habit, in just 30 days. This will give you the mindset and approach you can take on as you build your new routine.

Phase One: Unbearable (Days 1–10)

Phase One is when any new activity requires the largest amount of conscious effort, and getting up earlier than you have done is no different. You're fighting existing habits, the very habits that have been entrenched in *who you are* for years.

In this phase, it's mind over matter—and if you don't mind, it'll definitely matter! The habit of hitting the snooze button and not making the most of your day are habits that hold you back from becoming the superstar entrepreneur you have always known you can be. So dig in and hold strong.

In Phase One, while you battle existing patterns and limiting beliefs, you'll find out what you're made of and what you're capable of. You need to keep pushing, stay committed to your vision, and hang in there. Trust me when I say you can do this!

I know it can be daunting on day five to realize you still have twenty-five days to go before your transformation is complete and you've become a bona fide morning person. Keep in mind that on day five, you're actually more than halfway through the first phase and well on your way. Remember that your initial feelings are not going to last forever. In fact, you owe it to yourself to persevere because, in no time at all, you'll be getting the exact results you want as you become the person you've always wanted to be!

Phase Two: Uncomfortable (Days 11–20)

In Phase Two, your body and mind begin to acclimate to waking up earlier. You'll notice that getting up starts to get easier, but it's not yet a habit—it's not quite who you are and likely doesn't feel natural.

The biggest temptation at this level is to reward yourself by taking a break, especially on the weekends. A question posted quite often in the Miracle Morning Community is, "How many days a week do you get up early for your Miracle Morning?" Our answer—and the one that's most common from longtime Miracle Morning practitioners—is *every single day.*

Once you've made it through Phase One, you're past the hardest period. So keep going! Why on earth would you want to go through that first phase again by taking one or two days off? Trust me, you wouldn't, so don't!

Phase Three: Unstoppable (Days 21–30)

Early rising is now not only a habit, but it has literally become part of *who you are*, part of your identity. Your body and mind will have become accustomed to your new way of being. These next ten days are important for cementing the habit in yourself and your life.

As you engage in the Miracle Morning practice, you will also develop an appreciation for the three distinct phases of habit change. A side benefit is you will realize that you can identify, develop, and adopt any habit that serves you—including the habits of exceptional entrepreneur that we have included in this book.

Now that you've learned the simplest and most effective strategy for successfully implementing and sustaining any new habit in 30 days, you know the mindset and approach that you need to complete the Miracle Morning 30-Day Transformation Challenge. All that's required is for you to commit to get started and follow through.

Consider the Rewards

When you commit to the Miracle Morning 30-Day Transformation Challenge, you will be building a foundation for success in every area of your life for the rest of your life. By waking up each morning and practicing the Miracle Morning, you will begin each day with extraordinary levels of *discipline* (the crucial ability to get yourself to follow through with your commitments), *clarity* (the power you'll generate from focusing on what's most important), and *personal development* (perhaps the single most significant determining factor in your success). Thus, in the next 30 days, you'll find yourself quickly *becoming the person* you need to be to create the extraordinary levels of personal, professional, and financial success you truly desire.

You'll also be transforming the Miracle Morning from a concept that you may be excited (and possibly a little nervous) to *try* into a lifelong habit, one that will continue to develop you into the person you need to be to create the life you've always wanted. You'll begin to fulfill your potential and see results in your life far beyond what you've ever experienced before.

In addition to developing successful habits, you'll be developing the *mindset* you need to improve your life—both internally and externally. By practicing the Life S.A.V.E.R.S. each day, you'll be experiencing the physical, intellectual, emotional, and spiritual benefits of **S**ilence, **A**ffirmations, **V**isualization, **E**xercise, **R**eading, and **S**cribing. You'll immediately feel less stressed, more centered, focused, happier, and more excited about your life. You'll generate more energy, clarity and motivation to move toward your highest goals and dreams (especially those you've been putting off for far too long).

Remember, your life situation will improve after—but only *after*—you develop yourself into the person you need to be to improve it. That's exactly what these next 30 days of your life can be—a new beginning, and a new you.

You Can Do This!

If you're feeling nervous, hesitant, or concerned about whether you will be able to follow through with this for 30 days, relax—it's completely normal to feel that way. This is especially true if waking up in the morning is something you've found challenging in the past. It's not only expected that you would be a bit hesitant or nervous, but it's actually a very good sign! It's a sign that you're *ready* to commit, otherwise you wouldn't be nervous.

Here we go …

— BONUS CHAPTER —

THE MIRACLE EQUATION AND
THE ENTREPRENEURIAL SUCCESS FORMAULA

There are only two ways to live your life.
One is though nothing is a miracle.
The other is though everything is a miracle.
—ALBERT EINSTEIN

The Miracle Morning is about elevating yourself so that you can elevate your success. Now, it's time to take everything you've learned so far, and combine it with two of the ultimate success formulas, which nearly ALL top achievers—in every field—use to consistently expand what's possible.

When Hal and I got together to co-author this book, we began comparing notes and discussing the various philosophies and strategies that we've used and often share with other entrepreneurs. When

I learned about Hal's Miracle Equation, I realized how similar, yet complimentary, it is to the Entrepreneurial Success Formula that I teach. So, you're in luck … you get both!

First, I've asked Hal to share the Miracle Equation with you, and then I'll follow up with the Entrepreneurial Success Formula. You'll be able to implement either, or both, to further elevate your results.

The Miracle Equation

UF x EE = M

Hal here. Hope you're enjoying your Miracle Mornings! You know now that you can wake up early and accelerate your personal development with the Life S.A.V.E.R.S., maintain extraordinary levels of energy and unwavering focus throughout the day, and continuously develop and implement the entrepreneur's elevation skills and principles. But I know you didn't read this far merely to take your success up a notch. You want to make quantum leaps and generate extraordinary results, right? Right. If you also apply what follows to your career as an entrepreneur, you're going to go much further: you're going to join the elite performers—*the top one percent.*

To make those leaps, there is one more crucial strategy that you must add to your business toolbox, and it's called The Miracle Equation.

The Miracle Equation is the underlying strategy I used to consistently break sales records, become one of the youngest individuals ever inducted into my company's hall of fame, and go on to become a number one best-selling author and international keynote speaker. But it's more than that. It is precisely the same equation that ALL top performers—that top one percent—have used to create awe-inspiring results, while the other 99 percent wonder how they do it.

The Miracle Equation was born during one of my Cutco "push periods"—a 14-day span during which the company fostered friendly competition and created incentives to bring in record sales, both for the salesperson and the office.

This particular push period was special for two reasons. First, I was trying to become the first sales representative in company history to take the number one spot for three consecutive push periods. Second, I'd have to do it while being able to work only 10 of the 14 days.

I knew I needed to dig deep to achieve such a feat and that fear and self-doubt were a much greater hurdle than usual. In fact, I considered lowering my sales goal based on the circumstances. Then I remembered what one of my mentors, Dan Casetta, had taught me: "The true purpose of a goal isn't to hit the goal. The true purpose is to develop yourself into the type of person who can achieve your goals, regardless of whether you hit that particular one or not. It is who you become by giving it everything you have until the last moment—regardless of your results—that matters most."

I made a decision to stick with my original goal, even though the possibility of failing to achieve it was a real risk based on the limited time frame. With only 10 days to set a record, I knew I needed to be especially focused, faithful, and intentional. It was an ambitious objective, no question, and as you'll see, one that required me to dig deep and find out what I was really capable of.

The Two Decisions That Make the Impossible Possible

As with any great challenge, I needed to make decisions related to achieving the goal. I reverse-engineered the push period by asking myself, "If I were to break the record in just ten days, what decisions would I have to make now and commit to in advance?"

I identified the two decisions that would make the biggest impact. Only later did I realize that these were *the same two decisions that all top-performers make at some point in their lives.*

Those two decisions became the basis for the Miracle Equation.

The First Decision: Unwavering Faith

Knowing that I was already facing fear and self-doubt, I realized that to achieve the seemingly impossible, I would have to decide to maintain unwavering faith each and every day, *regardless of my results*. I knew that there would be moments when I would doubt myself and times when I would be so far off track that the goal would no longer seem achievable. But it would be those moments when I would have to override self-doubt with unshakeable faith.

To keep that level of faith in those challenging moments, I repeated what I call the Miracle Mantra:

I will _____ (make the next sale, call 20 prospects, reach my goal, etc.), no matter what—there is no other option.

Repeating this to myself, over and over again, served to program my subconscious mind while directing my conscious thinking, to get me to keep moving toward my goal.

Understand that maintaining unwavering faith is not *normal*. It's not natural. And that is why it's only practiced by the elite in any field. One of the challenges with maintaining unwavering faith that it doesn't always feel authentic because we have no way of knowing *for sure* if it's going to work. That's why they call it faith. It's one of the core components of what makes them elite. Elite athletes are one of the best examples of individuals who live by the Miracle Equation and maintain unwavering faith that they can win every game and make every shot they take—even though almost no athlete wins every game, and absolutely no athlete makes every shot.

Growing up, I was a huge fan of Michael Jordan, one of the greatest basketball players who has ever lived. Jordan exemplified the Miracle Equation, maintaining unwavering faith that he could make every shot he took. If he missed a shot, he wanted the ball again, because he knew that he could make the next shot. And if he missed two shots in a row, he wanted the ball again, because he maintained unwavering faith that he'd make his third shot. And if he missed the third shot, he wanted the ball again, because he knew he'd make the fourth.

See, the best athletes in the world want the ball, again and again, because at some point in their lives they made a decision—whether consciously or unconsciously—that they could make every shot they took, no matter how many shots they missed, even though the possibility of missing is always present and ultimately inevitable.

Whereas for the average athlete, missing a shot, or a few in a row, shook their confidence and caused their faith in themselves, and their abilities, to waiver. But not Jordan. No matter how many shots he missed, he always maintained unwavering faith that he'd make the *next* one.

Even when the game is on the line, and their team is down on the scorecards, and there are only seconds left, it is the elite performers—the Michael Jordans of the world—who, without hesitation, tell their team, "Give me the ball." The rest of the team breathes a sigh of relief because they fear that they might miss the game-winning shot, while Michael Jordan enters into every shot with unwavering faith, despite the fact that he might miss. In fact, during his legendary career, Jordan missed 26 game-winning shots, and only made 22. His faith that he would make every single one never wavered.

That's the first decision that the world's elite make, and it's yours for the making, too.

When you're working toward a goal and you're not on track, what is the first thing that goes out the window? *The faith that reaching the goal is possible.* Your self-talk becomes, *I'm not on track. It doesn't look like I'm going to reach my goal.* And with each passing moment, your faith decreases, and you're consumed with self-doubt.

That faith—and the faith you need to develop—isn't based on probability. It draws from a whole different place. Most entrepreneurs and businesses operate based on what is known as the *law of averages.* But what we're talking about here is the *law of miracles.* When you miss shot after shot—in your case, sale after sale—you have to tell yourself what Michael Jordan tells himself, *I've missed three, but I want the ball next, and I'm going to make that next shot.*

You don't have to settle for the law of averages. You have the ability and the choice to maintain that same unwavering faith, no matter what, regardless of the results. You may sometimes doubt yourself or have a bad day, but you must actively choose—and re-choose—to maintain unwavering faith that all things are possible, and hold it throughout your journey, whether it is a 10-day push period or a 30-year career.

When it doesn't look like the desired result is likely, average performers give up the faith that the result is possible.

You will repeat the Miracle Mantra to yourself:

I will _____ (sign up the next prospect, call 20 prospects, reach my goal), no matter what. There is no other option.

Then, you simply uphold your integrity and do what it is you say you are going to do.

An elite athlete may be having the worst game ever, where it seems as if, in the first three-quarters of the game, they can't make a shot to save their life. Yet in the fourth quarter, right when the team needs them, they start making those shots. They always want the ball; they always have belief and faith in themselves. In the fourth quarter, they score three times as many shots as they've made in the first three-quarters of the game.

Why? They have conditioned themselves to have unwavering faith in their talents, skills, and abilities, regardless of what it says on the scoreboard or their stats sheet.

And …

They combine their unwavering faith with part two of the Miracle Equation: extraordinary effort.

The Second Decision: Extraordinary Effort

When you allow your faith to go out the window, effort almost always follows right behind it. *After all,* you tell yourself, *what's the point in even trying to make the sale or achieve your goal if it's not possible?* Suddenly, you find yourself wondering how you're ever going to find the next new marketer or sell another product, let alone reach the big goal you've been working toward.

I've been there many times, feeling deflated, thinking, *what's the point of even trying?* As an entrepreneur, if you're halfway through a month, and you should be at $50,000, but you're only at $7,500, you begin to think *There's no way I can make it.*

That's where extraordinary effort comes into play. You need to stay focused on your original goal—you need to connect to the vision you had for it, that big *why* you had in your heart and mind when you set the goal in the first place.

Like me, you need to reverse engineer the goal. Ask yourself, *If I'm at the end of this month and this goal were to have happened, what would I have done? What would I have needed to do?*

Whatever the answer, you will need to take massive action and give it everything you have, regardless of your results. You have to believe you can still ring the bell of success at the end. You have to maintain unwavering faith and extraordinary effort—until the buzzer sounds. That's the only way that you create an opportunity for the miracle to happen.

If you do what the average person does—what our built-in human nature tells us to do—you'll be just like every other average entrepreneur. Don't choose to be that average person! Remember: your thoughts and actions become a self-fulfilling prophecy.

Allow me to introduce you to your edge—the strategy that, when you use it, will skyrocket your goals and practically ensure every one of your ambitions is realized.

The Miracle Equation

Unwavering Faith + Extraordinary Effort = Miracles

It's easier than you think. The secret to maintaining unwavering faith is to recognize that it's a mindset and a *strategy*—it's not concrete. In fact, it's elusive. You can never make *every* sale. No athlete makes *every* shot. So, you have to program yourself to automatically have the unwavering faith to drive you to keep putting forth the extraordinary effort.

Remember, the key to putting this equation into practice, to maintaining unwavering faith in the midst of self-doubt, is *The Miracle Mantra*:

I will _____, no matter what. There is no other option.

For me, recently, it was "I will generate $1.5 million in revenue, no matter what. There is no other option."

Once you set a goal, insert that goal into the Miracle Mantra format. Yes, you're going to say your affirmations every morning (and maybe every evening, too). But all day, every day, you're going to repeat your Miracle Mantra to yourself. As you're driving or taking the train to the office, while you're on the treadmill, in the shower, in line at the grocery store, driving to pick up a prospect—in other words, *everywhere you go.*

Your Miracle Mantra will fortify your faith and be the self-talk you need to make just one more call or talk to one more person as they come through the door.

Bonus Lesson

Remember what I learned from my mentor, Dan Casetta: *The purpose of a goal isn't to hit the goal. The real purpose is to develop yourself into the type of person who can achieve your goals, regardless of whether you hit that particular one or not. It is who you become, by giving it everything you have until the last moment—regardless of your results—that matters most.*

You have to become the type of person who *can* achieve the goal. You won't always reach the goal, but you can become someone who maintains unwavering faith and puts forth extraordinary effort, regardless of your results. That's how you become the type of person you need to become to consistently achieve extraordinary goals.

And while reaching the goal almost doesn't matter (almost!), more often than not, you'll reach your goal. Do the elite athletes win every time? No. But they win most of the time. And you'll win most of the time, too.

At the end of the day, you can wake up earlier, do the Life S.A.V.E.R.S. with passion and excitement, get organized, focused, and intentional, and master every sales technique like a champ. And yet, if you don't combine unwavering faith with extraordinary effort, you won't reach the levels of sales success you seek.

The Miracle Equation gives you access to forces outside of anyone's understanding, using an energy that I might call God, the Universe, the Law of Attraction, or even good luck. I don't know *how* it works; I just know *that* it works.

You've read this far—you clearly want success more than almost anything. Commit to following through with every aspect of entrepreneurship, including the Miracle Equation. You deserve it, and I want you to have it!

Putting It into Action:

1. Write out the Miracle Equation and put it where you will see it every day: **Unwavering Faith + Extraordinary Effort = Miracles (UF + EE = M∞)**

2. What's your #1 goal for this year? What goal, if you were to accomplish it, would take your success to a whole new level?

3. Write your Miracle Mantra: *I will _____ (insert your goals and daily actions, here), no matter what. There is no other option.*

It is more about who you become in the process. You'll expand your self-confidence and, regardless of your results, the very next time you attempt to reach a goal, and every time after that, you'll be the type of person who gives it all they've got.

The Entrepreneurial Success Formula
F x F x E = S

It's Cameron, again, for this last, final stretch. Stay with me, you're going to get a rich nugget here. The secret formula for calculating the chance of entrepreneurial success is very similar to the formula Hal used in the Miracle Equation. The one I use, the Entrepreneurial Success Formula is *F x F x E = S*.

The first F is for *Focus*. The second F is for *Faith*. The E represents *Effort*, and the S stands for Success. So, your *Focus* multiplied by your *Faith* multiplied by your *Effort* equals your level of *Success*. And it's actually quite mathematically interesting.

To truly be successful as an entrepreneur, you need to have all three of these areas cranking.

The way it works is on a yearly, quarterly, monthly, weekly, or even daily basis, entrepreneurs should assess and write down the following:

1. On a scale of 0 percent to 100 percent, how *focused* are you on the activities that are responsible for driving and growing your business? Those can include reviewing key metrics and

data (daily or weekly)? Connecting with and managing your team? How truly focused are you on reviewing your core goals and tracking your progress against them? How focused are you on executing what really matters, day to day? Are you scattered? Do you get sucked into social media, or are you focused on getting the highest impact projects completed? Again, on a scale of 0 percent to 100 percent, give yourself an honest assessment. Day to day, are you 40 percent focused on high level activities? Fifty percent? Eighty percent? Ninety percent? Write down that number, and keep it where you can see it.

2.   How much *faith* do you have in yourself and your business? You know, faith in the fact that you have the right team, faith in your market, faith in your product, faith in your future … or are you second-guessing yourself? Do you wake up in the morning and think *Yeah, I've got it all pretty good, and I know what we're doing, and I feel comfortable and confident?* Or are you nervous, fearful, and worried? Faith is a product of your confidence. How much faith do you have in your team, in your product, in your service, and in what you're doing? How much faith do you have in your own skill set to do the job of entrepreneur? What percent faith do you have, from zero through 100 percent. Forty percent faith? Fifty percent? Eighty percent? Ninety percent? Write that number down too.

3.   Lastly, it's about *effort*. What percent effort are you putting in? Are you putting in 100 percent effort, or are you putting in 50 percent? Are you putting in long, solid, hard days, or are you winging it and shooting from the hip? Are you seriously sitting down at your desk and cranking? Are you wasting time throughout the days and weeks? What percent effort are you putting in, on a percentage basis from zero through 100 percent. Sixty percent effort? Seventy percent? Eighty percent? Ninety percent? Write that number down.

Now, this is where the magic of this secret formula actually kicks in for you. You take your percentages from each of three areas, focus, faith and effort, and you multiply them. The result is your Chance of Success as an Entrepreneur.

- Entrepreneurial Success Formula
- Focus x Faith x Effort = Success
- F x F x E = Success
- ____% x ____% x ____% = ____% Chance of Success

Take for example, an entrepreneur running their company who was 80 percent focused, had 80 percent faith, and was putting in an 80 percent effort into things would normally think they are kicking ass. However, look how the numbers actually stack up.

- F x F x E = Success
- ____% x ____% x ____% = ____% Chance of Success
- 80% x 80% x 80% = 51.2% Chance of Success

Those aren't very good odds. In fact, I've told clients with similar numbers that they'd be better off going to Vegas and putting 100 percent of their available cash on the wheel, picking red or black, and betting it all on one spin. They'd save themselves a ton of stress too.

Even if a client was doing better, let's say 90 percent focused, 90 percent faith, and 90 percent effort, their numbers are not that awesome either.

- 90% x 90% x 90% = 72.9% Chance of Success

The reality is, if entrepreneurs want to be successful, they need to ratchet up those numbers. They need 98% numbers—or at least I do.

- 98% x 98% x 98% = 94.1% Chance of Success

Those are odds worth betting on. And frankly, starting your days with a Miracle Morning mindset and system will set you and your company on the path to success.

Here is how I use this formula to guide and motivate me ...

Quarterly, monthly, weekly, and occasionally daily, I quickly write down the numbers and see how I'm doing ... As I write this book, here are mine related to my new COO Alliance ...

- F x F x E = Success
- 90% x 95% x 90% = 76.9% Chance of Success

Not good enough, so it's time to grow each of those three numbers as it relates to that core business focus.

Where are you with your core business focus?

Closing Remarks

Congratulations! You have done what only a small percentage of people do: read an entire book. If you've come this far, that tells me something about you: you have a thirst for more. You want to become more, do more, contribute more, and earn more.

Right now, you have the unprecedented opportunity to infuse the Life S.A.V.E.R.S. into your daily life and business, upgrade your daily routine, and ultimately upgrade your *life* to a first class experience beyond your wildest dreams. Before you know it, you will be reaping the astronomical benefits of the habits that top achievers use daily.

Five years from now, your life, business, relationships, and income will be a direct result of one thing: *who you've become*. It's up to you to wake up each day and dedicate time to becoming the best version of yourself. Seize this moment in time, define a vision for your future, and use what you've learned in this book to turn your vision into your reality.

Imagine a time just a few years from now when you come across the journal you started after completing this book. In it, you find the goals you wrote down for yourself—dreams you didn't even dare speak out loud at the time. And as you look around, you realize *your dreams from that time now represent the life you are living.*

Right now, you stand at the foot of a mountain you can easily and effortlessly climb. All you need to do is continue waking up each day for your Miracle Morning and use the Life S.A.V.E.R.S. day after day, month after month, year after year, as you continue to take your *self*, your *business*, and your *success* to levels beyond what you've ever experienced before.

Combine your Miracle Morning with a commitment to master your Entrepreneurship Skills and Not-So-Obvious Principles, and use the Miracle Equation to create results that most people only dream of.

This book was written as an expression of what Hal and I know will work for you, to take every area of your life to the next level, faster than you may currently believe is possible. Miraculous performers weren't born that way—they have simply dedicated their lives to developing themselves and their skills to achieve everything they've ever wanted.

You can become one of them, I promise.

Taking Action: The 30-Day Miracle Morning Challenge

Now it is time to join the tens of thousands of people who have transformed their lives, incomes, and entrepreneurial careers with *The Miracle Morning*. Join the community online at TMMBook.com and download the toolkit to get you started *today*.

Four Steps to Begin the Miracle Morning (30-Day) Transformation Challenge

---

Step 1: Get the Miracle Morning 30-Day Transformation Challenge Fast Start Kit

Visit www.TMMBook.com to download your free Miracle Morning 30-Day Transformation Challenge Fast Start Kit—complete with the exercises, affirmations, daily checklists, tracking sheets, and everything else you need to make starting and completing the Miracle Morning 30-Day Transformation Challenge as easy as possible. Please take a minute to do this now.

Step 2: Plan Your First Miracle Morning for Tomorrow

If you haven't already begun, commit to and schedule your first Miracle Morning as soon as possible—ideally *tomorrow*. Yes, actually write it in your schedule and decide where you will do it. Remember it's recommended that you leave your bedroom to remove yourself from the temptations of your bed altogether. My Miracle Morning takes place every day on my living room couch while everyone else in my house is still sound asleep. I've heard from people who do their Miracle Morning sitting outside in nature, on their porch or deck, or at a nearby park. Do yours where you feel most comfortable, but also where you won't be interrupted.

Step 3: Read Page 1 of the Fast Start Kit and Do the Exercises

Read the introduction in your Miracle Morning 30-Day Life Transformation Challenge Fast Start Kit then follow the instructions and complete the exercises. Like anything in life that's worthwhile, successfully completing the Miracle Morning 30-Day Life Transformation Challenge requires a bit of preparation. It's important that you do the initial exercises in your Fast Start Kit (which shouldn't take you more than 30–60 minutes), and keep in mind that your Miracle Morning will always start with the *preparation* you do the day or night before to get yourself ready mentally, emotionally, and logistically for the Miracle Morning. This preparation includes following the steps in the Five-Step, Snooze-Proof, Wake-Up Strategy in chapter 2.

Step 4: Get an Accountability Partner (Recommended)

The overwhelming evidence for the correlation between success and accountability is undeniable. While most people resist being held accountable, having someone who will hold us to higher standards than we'll hold ourselves to makes a huge impact on our ability to do what we set out to do. All of us can benefit from the support of an accountability partner, so it's highly recommended —but definitely not required—that you reach out to someone in your circle of influence (famliy, friend, colleague, significant other, etc.)

and enlist their support for the Miracle Morning 30-Day Life Transformation Challenge.

Not only does having someone to hold us accountable increase the odds we will follow through, but joining forces with someone else is simply more fun! Consider that when you're excited about something and committed to doing it on your own, there is a certain level of power in that excitement and your individual commitment. However, when you have someone else who is as excited about and committed to it as you are, it's much more powerful.

Call, text, or email someone (or more than one!) today, and invite them to join you for The Miracle Morning 30-Day Life Transformation Challenge. The quickest way to get them up to speed is to send them the link to www.MiracleMorning.com so they can get free and immediate access to the Miracle Morning Fast Start Kit, which contains the following:

- **The FREE Miracle Morning Video training**
- **The FREE Miracle Morning Audio training**
- **Two FREE Chapters of *The Miracle Morning* book**

It will cost them nothing, and you'll be teaming up with someone who is also committed to taking their life to the next level, so the two of you can support and encourage each other as well as hold yourselves accountable.

IMPORTANT: Don't wait until you have an accountability partner on board to do your first Miracle Morning and start the 30-Day Life Transformation Challenge. Whether you've found someone to embark on the journey with you, I still recommend scheduling and doing your first *Miracle Morning* tomorrow—no matter what. Don't wait. You'll be even more capable of inspiring someone else to do the Miracle Morning with you if you've already experienced a few days of it. Get started. Then, as soon as you can, invite a friend, family member, or co-worker to visit www.MiracleMorning.com to get their free Miracle Morning Fast Start Kit.

In less than an hour, they'll be fully capable of being your *Miracle Morning* accountability partner—and probably a little inspired.

Are You Ready to Take Your Life to the Next Level?

What is the next level in your personal or professional life? Which areas need to be transformed for you to reach that level? Give yourself the gift of investing only 30 days to make significant improvements in your life, one day at a time. No matter what your past has been, you *can* change your future by changing the present.

Entrepreneur Profile

Pat Flynn

Pat Flynn's company is Smart Passive Income.

Top Business Accomplishments

❖ Pat is the *Wall Street Journal* Best-Selling Author of *Will It Fly*.

❖ In 2015, he received the Best Business Podcast Award from Academy of Podcasters.

❖ He is an advisor for Companies like LeadPages, ConvertKit, and Pencils of Promise.

❖ Pat has been featured in *Forbes* Magazine as a Top Transparent Business Leader.

❖ He has more than 30 million downloads for his podcasts.

Morning Routine

❖ Pat gets up at 4:00 a.m. to wash his face and brush teeth.

❖ He drinks eight ounces of water and eats toasted Ezekiel bread with almond butter.

❖ He stretches and does visualizations focused on what he'd like to accomplish during the day.

❖ Then he heads to the basketball gym three days a week. On the other two, he works or writes instead.

❖ He does seven minutes of meditation and five minutes of journaling (using *The Five Minute Journal*).

❖ Then he reads his affirmations followed by reading until his kids get up.

❖ He hangs out with his kids and prepares them for school.

❖ He and his wife take his son to school.

❖ Then he spends time with his wife and daughter, playing games, reading and enjoying the rest of the day!

— CONCLUSION —

LET TODAY BE THE DAY YOU GIVE UP WHO YOU'VE BEEN FOR WHO YOU CAN BECOME

Every day, think as you wake up, "Today I am fortunate to have woken up, I am alive, I have a precious human life, I am not going to waste it. I am going to use all my energies to develop myself, to expand my heart out to others. I am going to benefit others as much as I can."
—DALAI LAMA

Things do not change. We change.
—HENRY DAVID THOREAU

Where you are is a result of who you *were*, but where you go from here depends entirely on who you choose to be from this moment forward.

Now is your time. Decide that today is the most important day of your life because it is who you are becoming *now*—based on the choices that you make, and the actions that you take—which will determine who and where you are going to be for the rest of your life. Don't put off creating and experiencing the life—happiness, health, wealth, success, and love—that you truly want and deserve.

As Kevin Bracy, one of my mentors, always urged, "Don't wait to be great." If you want your life to improve, you have to improve yourself first. You can download the Miracle Morning 30-Day Life Transformation Fast-Start Kit at www.TMMBook.com. Then, with or without an accountability partner, commit to complete your 30-day challenge so that you will immediately begin accessing more of your potential than you ever have before. Imagine ... just one month from now, you will be well on your way to transforming every area of your life.

Let's Keep Helping Others

May I ask you a quick favor?

If this book has added value to your life, if you feel like you're better off after reading it, and you see that the Miracle Morning can be a new beginning for you to take any, or every, area of your life to the next level, I'm hoping you'll do something for someone you care about:

Give this book to them or let them borrow your copy. Ask them to read it so that they have the opportunity to transform their life for the better too. Or, if you're not willing to give up your copy quite yet because you're planning to reread it, you could get them their own copy for no reason other than to say, "Hey, I love and appreciate you, and I want to help you live your best life. Read this."

If you believe as I do that being a great friend (or family member) is about helping your friends and loved ones to become the best versions of themselves, I encourage you to share this book with them.

Together, we are truly elevating the consciousness of humanity, one morning at a time.

Thank you so much.

A SPECIAL INVITATION FROM HAL

Readers and practitioners of *The Miracle Morning* have co-created an extraordinary community consisting of over 200,000 like-minded individuals from around the world who wake up each day with purpose and dedicate time to fulfilling the unlimited potential that is within all of us, while helping others to do the same.

As author of *The Miracle Morning*, I felt I had a responsibility to create an online community where readers could come together to connect, get encouragement, share best practices, support one another, discuss the book, post videos, find accountability partners, and even swap smoothie recipes and exercise routines.

However, I honestly had no idea that The Miracle Morning Community would become one of the most positive, engaged, and supportive online communities in the world—but it has. I'm constantly astounded by the caliber and character of our membership, which presently includes people from over 70 countries and is growing daily.

Just go to **www.MyTMMCommunity.com** and request to join The Miracle Morning Community on Facebook®. You'll immediately be able to connect with 80,000+ people who are already practicing TMM. While you'll find many who are just beginning their Miracle Morning journey, you'll discover even more who have been at it for years and who will happily share advice and guidance to accelerate your success.

I'll be moderating the Community and checking in regularly, so I look forward to seeing you there! If you'd like to reach out to me personally on social media, follow **@HalElrod** on Twitter and **Facebook.com/YoPalHal** on Facebook. Let's connect soon!

ABOUT THE AUTHORS

HAL ELROD is one of the highest-rated keynote speakers in America as evidenced by his average of 9.7 out of 10.0 rating across multiple Entrepreneur Organization (EO) chapters. However, he's still best known as the author of what is now being widely regarded as one of the most life-changing books ever written (with 1,500+ five-star reviews on Amazon), *The Miracle Morning: The Not-So-Obvious Secret Guaranteed to Transform Your Life (Before 8AM)*, which has also been translated into 21 languages and is a bestseller around the world.

The seed for Hal's life's work was planted at age 20, when Hal was found dead at the scene of a horrific car accident. Hit head-on by a drunk driver at 70 miles per hour, he broke 11 bones, died for six minutes, and suffered permanent brain damage. After six days in a coma, he woke to face his unimaginable reality—which included being told by doctors that he would never walk again. Defying the logic of doctors, and proving that all of us are capable of overcoming even seemingly insurmountable adversity to achieve anything we set our minds to, Hal went on to not only walk, but to run a 52-mile ultramarathon, become a hall of fame business achiever, international best-selling author, keynote speaker, and host of the top-rated *Achieve Your Goals* podcast on iTunes.

Most importantly, Hal is beyond grateful to now be married to the woman of his dreams and the father of two, sharing his life with his wife and their two children in Austin, Texas.

For more information on Hal's keynote speaking, live events, coaching, books, and the soon-to-be released *Miracle Morning Movie* (documentary), visit www.HalElrod.com.

CAMERON HEROLD is known around the world as the Business Growth Guru.

He is the mastermind behind hundreds of companies' exponential growth. Cameron's built a dynamic consultancy—his current clients include a "Big 4" wireless carrier and a monarchy. What do his clients say they like most about him? He isn't a theory guy—they like that Cameron speaks only from experience. He earned his reputation as the business growth guru by guiding his clients to double their profit and revenue in three years or less.

Cameron was an entrepreneur from day one. At age 21, he had 14 employees. By 35, he'd help build his first two *$100 million* companies. By the age of 42, Cameron engineered 1-800-GOT-JUNK?'s spectacular growth from $2 million to $106 million in revenue, and 3100 employees—and he did that in only six years. His companies landed over 5,200 media placements in that same period, including coverage on Oprah.

Not only does Cameron know how to grow businesses, but his delivery from the stage is second to none—the current publisher of Forbes magazine, Rich Karlgaard, said, "Cameron Herold is THE BEST SPEAKER I've ever heard … he hits grand slams."

When Cameron steps off the stage, he doesn't stop teaching. He is the author of the global best-selling business book *Double Double,* which is in its 7th printing and in multiple translations around the world.

Cameron is a top-rated international speaker and has been paid to speak in 26 countries. He is also the top-rated lecturer at EO/MIT's Entrepreneurial Master's program and a powerful and effective speaker at Chief Executive Officer and Chief Operating Officer leadership events around the world.

Look for Cameron's three new business books on public relations, meetings, and how to get your team to see your vision for your company, releasing in 2016.

HONORÉE CORDER is the author of dozens of books, including *You Must Write a Book, Vision to Reality, The Prosperous Writer* book series, *Business Dating, The Successful Single Mom* book series, *If Divorce is a Game, These are the Rules,* and *The Divorced Phoenix.* She is also Hal Elrod's business partner in *The Miracle Morning* book series. Honorée coaches business professionals, writers, and aspiring non-fiction authors who want to publish their books to bestseller status, create a platform, and develop multiple streams of income. She also does all sorts of other magical things, and her badassery is legendary. You can find out more at HonoreeCorder.com.

THE MIRACLE MORNING SERIES

The Journal

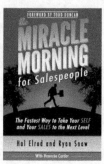

for Salespeople

for Real Estate Agents

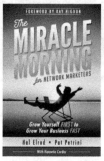

for Network Marketers

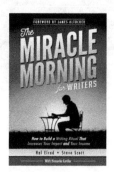

for Writers

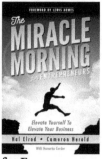

for Entrepreneurs

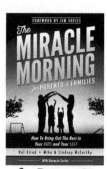

for Parents & Families

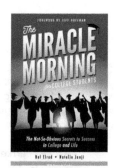

for College Students

COMPANION GUIDES & WORKBOOKS

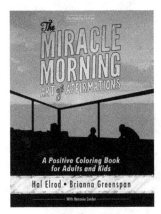

Art of Affirmations

**for Network Marketers
90-Day Action Plan**

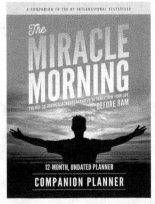

Companion Planner

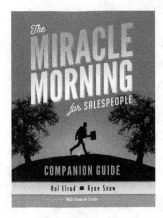

**for Salespeople
Companion Guide**

**for College Students
Companion Planner**

HAL ELROD & JON BERGHOFF

PRESENT...

ONE WEEKEND CAN CHANGE YOUR LIFE.
JOIN US FOR THIS ONCE-IN-A-LIFETIME EXPERIENCE.

www.BestYearEverLive.com

Most personal development events cause "information overload" and often leave attendees feeling more overwhelmed than when they arrived. You end up with pages and pages of notes, then you go home and have to figure out how and when to implement everything you've learned.

Co-hosted by experiential trainer, Jon Berghoff, the **Best Year Ever Blueprint LIVE** event won't just teach you how to change your life, you'll actually starting taking steps to *change your life while you're still at the event*.

"I truly had a life changing weekend during BYEB2015. I feel as if my mind has hit a 'reset' button. Reading The Miracle Morning and coming to the live event has been a gift, and the best investment in myself I've ever made. I am excited to take this momentum and create my level 10 life next year!"

Ericka Staples

Learn more about the Best Year Ever event online at
WWW.BESTYEAREVERLIVE.COM

CPSIA information can be obtained
at www.ICGtesting.com
Printed in the USA
LVHW04s2334290818
588617LV00009B/136/P

9 781942 589129